# How to Collect
# Great Art on a Shoestring

David L. Gersh

Published by Open Books

Copyright © 2019 by David L. Gersh

All rights reserved. No part of this book may be reproduced, scanned, or distributed in any printed or electronic form without permission except in the case of brief quotations embodied in critical articles and reviews.

Interior design by Siva Ram Maganti

Cover images © Chamille White shutterstock.com/g/chamille

ISBN-13: 978-1948598149

A simple piece of advice borrowed from Abbie Hoffman: "Steal this book!"— **Paul Hayes Tucker, art historian and curator, Paul Hayes Tucker Distinguished Professor of Art, Emeritus, University of Massachusetts Boston**

David Gersh has written a book that is wise, articulate, and dare I say funny. This is clearly a true passion for the author and will ignite, with a guiding hand, how you can actually bring great art into your life. — **Noah benShea, International Best Selling Author and Philosopher**

David Gersh simplifies one of the world's more esoteric pastimes. His knowledgeable account of collecting art is interspersed with delightful anecdotes about artists and collectors, making this a treasure.— **Kathleen Sharp, award-winning author of Mr. & Mrs. Hollywood: Edie and Lew Wasserman and Their Entertainment Empire**

Other Books by David L. Gersh

*Art Is Dead*
*Going, Going, Gone*
*Desperate Shop Girls*
*Art Attack*
*The Whisper of a Distant God*

For Anne

# Contents

| | |
|---|---|
| Prologue | ix |
| 1. The Auction: Selecting | 1 |
| 2. The Auction: Our Research | 5 |
| 3. The Auction: Bidding and Success | 7 |
| 4. What is Great Art? | 9 |
| 5. What is a Shoestring? | 13 |
| 6. Dead Artists | 17 |
| 7. Insecurity | 21 |
| 8. About Us | 25 |
| 9. Where to Look | 29 |
| 10. The Essentials | 35 |
| 11. Look for the Edge | 41 |
| 12. The Jungle: How to Select Art | 47 |
| 13. Tips on Research | 51 |
| 14. The Kinds of Art | 57 |
| 15. Prints and Multiples | 61 |
| 16. Bidding and Offers | 65 |
| 17. The Trend | 69 |
| 18. The Pricing of Contemporary Art | 73 |

| | |
|---|---|
| 19. What You Need to Know | 77 |
| 20. The Great Auction Houses | 85 |
| 21. The Art World | 91 |
| 22. A Brief Romp Through Recent Art History | 97 |
| 23. What is Art? | 103 |
| 24. Mistakes | 111 |
| 25. Owning Art | 115 |
| 26. Cataloging and Insurance | 119 |
| 27. Tales From the Jungle | 121 |
| 28. More Tales | 127 |
| 29. A Final Word | 133 |
| Acknowledgements | 134 |

# Prologue

Collecting art is a passion. The art world is opaque and secretive. Collecting requires knowledge and discipline. But, living with good art is special. Its feeling doesn't wane and it can bring joy every day.

This book explores a flaw in the art market that provides collectors, who have limited resources, the means to collect one-of-a-kind works by extraordinary artists.

There is always the new, new thing. The hot, young, sleek maverick of the moment who is the toast of the art world.

Tastes change and collectors have short memories. Unless there is a gallery actively pushing an artist's work, or, even perhaps, a museum retrospective, enumerable artists fall from the lips and minds of collectors and professionals. This is what creates opportunity.

Artists who had critical success, who were talented and devoted, who were handled by world renowned galleries and collected by major museums, have been forgotten. There are hundreds of them. You would not know their names. I certainly didn't. Even museum professionals who don't know them are delighted when they see their work.

Just a single example. I had never heard of Carmen Herrera. I had never seen her work. My wife, Anne, and I were in New York in 2017 and happened upon the Whitney retrospective, celebrating Herrera's 101st birthday. I was simply blown away. It was the first exhibition of her art in New York in over 20 years.

In the 1950s, Herrera developed a distilled geometric style of abstraction and reduced her palette to three colors for each composition. Her work emerged at the same time as that of Ellsworth Kelly, in a case of parallel development. Kelly became famous. Carmen Herrera was forgotten.

Herrera prefigured Minimalism by almost a decade. She didn't sell her first piece of art until 2004, when she was almost 90 years old. I wish I had bought it. I wish I had discovered her before anyone else. She is what this book is about.

In case you might think this oversight is limited to recent artists, the Frick Collection in New York is installing a major show of the Renaissance painter, Giovanni Battista Moroni, in the first major exhibition of his work in the United States. As *The New York Times* said, "The history of art is littered with significant painters who never reach the same level of renown as some of their peers. Sometimes omissions are justified by a disparity of skill, but in certain cases bad luck, prejudice or misunderstanding prevented artists from getting recognition."

---

After launching a probing assault on my teeth, my dentist decided to upgrade his dingy to a yacht. He left my art budget in a shambles. I had to find a new way to collect. It sent me in a different direction and on to some novel discoveries. Bless his heart.

I collect dead artists. That is bad for the artists, but good for me. Their body of work is set, both in quantity and quality. It allows research and the ability to qualify their art. The methods of doing so are my story. To be able to create a collection of original art of high quality on a limited budget is a grand adventure.

The art world is a jungle. It is largely unregulated. It is full of stunning flora and beautiful creatures. A glistening river of art flows through it. And predators hunt the unwary.

To perhaps peak your curiosity and to lure you into its beauty and shadows, I survey the ways and the scandals that exist within it. But once you enter this jungle, it will never loosen its grip on you.

In some ways, this book is a primer on collecting. There may be background material familiar to the more experienced collector. But it took me years of collecting to learn a lot of these things, so perhaps a review will be helpful.

In certain circles, collectors are seen as rich, privileged and powerful. Most of these, observed Loic Gouzer of Christie's, don't actually enjoy discussing art and asking questions. They see a Twombly painting and Gouzer will say, "You should compare it to others in Twombly's catalogue raisonne'." And they'll respond, "I just need to know if it's an A or an A+ or a B+."

If you are interested in this book, you are not rich. Only passionate or curious. Collecting is a lifelong journey. Goethe, the poet, wrote that the collector is a happy person. I believe he was right.

So, what is a "shoestring?" And what is "great art?" For that matter "What is art?"

For me, writing a book is the crossroads of hubris and humility. Hubris because I think someone will want to read what I have written. Humility because I fear no one will. So, I hope you read on. Or at least that you have already bought this book.

# Chapter 1

## THE AUCTION: SELECTING

ON MAY 5, 2018, RAGO Auctions in Lambertville, New Jersey, held a Post-War & Contemporary art auction. Anne and I collect abstract art with most of our collection centered on works from the mid-1970s. I had never heard of Rago Auctions until I started looking at Bidsquare. Bidsquare is an online local auction aggregator. It allowed me to find local auction houses I otherwise would have been unable to discover.

Rago has an online website. Like all auctions now, the entire catalog was free, online. There were 297 lots in the auction. I collect dead artists. It narrowed the selection.

Many works were wonderful. Some were prints, art produced in editions, in which I had no interest. And some were just uninteresting. A number were beyond my budget. But quite a few were not. Unlike many auctions, this auction was limited to art within the area we collect. That is one reason I was attracted to it.

I looked at every lot. Twice. The first time was a survey to understand the scope and quality of the art. Of course, some work jumped out at me. In the second review I closely looked at each lot. I wrote down the lot numbers that made me respond viscerally (because I believe emotion is the first step in appreciating a piece of art, particularly abstract art) and then discarded those lots with estimates beyond my budget.

I went back to review the catalog a third time after a few days. If I was distracted by the pieces that caught my eye, I may have missed some interesting work. In this case, I had not.

When I make a note of the art in which we are interested, I list the name of the artist, the auction (there may be several in which I am interested going on at the same time), the lot number in the auction, the type of art (oil on canvas, etc.), the birth and death dates of the artist, the date the art work was made and the sales estimate. All this information is available in the catalog and I use it to research the pieces I intend to pursue further.

I ultimately wanted to look more closely at five lots. I only wanted a one-of-a-kind piece (which I will refer to in this book as a "unique," as distinguished from an original work produced in a series, a "print"). Preferably on canvas. I was also constrained by my $5,000 budget, of which I had already spent about $2,600 on a Sonia Gechtoff acrylic on paper (more about that later). There were several more works I responded to, but put aside for various reasons.

I loved a Kenneth Noland (1924-2010) diamond-shaped painting (one of his iconic series). But at an estimate of $15,000-$20,000, it was out of my price range (it sold for $50,000 including the sales commission). Auction estimates do not include the 25% buyer's commission. It is added to the winning bid price (the "hammer price").

But sales results do include the commission. So, note, the Noland actually sold for $40,000 on the floor, but cost $50,000 with the commission and before sales tax.

There were two Theodoros Stamos (1922-1997) pieces I liked, but we already had a Theodoros Stamos in our collection and I did not want another. There was a wonderful Arshile Gorky (1904-1948) oil in the sale, but it was estimated at $50,000-$70,000 (and sold for $175,000 before tax. That is what can happen when a piece is fiercely desired by more than one bidder.) A Michael Goldberg (1924-2007) oil was a good piece and in my price range, but it didn't send off chimes and bells for me.

A Rollin Crampton (1886-1970) oil thrilled me. It had an estimate of $800-$1,200, which was also compelling. I was captured by a Pierre Lesieur (1922-2011) oil, estimated at $2,000-$3,000, and a Giorgio Cavallon (1904-1989) oil, estimated to sell at $8000-$12000 (I'm not as disciplined as I would like). I also responded to two paintings

## The Auction: Selecting

by Angelo Ippolito (1922-2001) (estimated at $1,200-$1,800 and $800-$1,200 respectively.) I didn't want both.

The Rollin Crampton was a fantastic work. Crampton is a widely collected artist. It made my mouth water, but the work was simply too large. We didn't have wall space. I recommended the piece to another collector with whom I exchange tips. He loved it and bid on it, but the piece sold for $4,375, notwithstanding its $800-$1,200 estimate.

I was pleased that my friend exercised bidding discipline. It is an important skill. I wasn't sure I could with that piece. Auctions are very competitive and they bring out the worst in me. My competitive juices flow. Without bidding discipline, you can hurt yourself financially. And at this level of art collecting, you are unlikely to recoup your purchase price upon resale because of the transaction costs and sales tax.

Alas, the Cavallon was beyond my reach financially. Besides it was only 14 inches by 12 inches, which is small for an abstract painting. I find that many smaller abstracts do not present well.

## Chapter 2

# THE AUCTION: OUR RESEARCH

So, there were two artists I needed to research, Lesieur and Ippolito. I had never heard of either of them.

I went to the internet. It's easy. The artist's website and Wikipedia are good places to start. If you use Wikipedia, be aware it may contain inaccurate information. Look at the footnotes and follow through with your research.

Often, for important artists, *The New York Times* will have an obituary. Such an obituary in itself lends credence to the stature of the artist.

I also looked at the back of the paintings. The lot images usually include both the front and back of the piece. Stickers on the back indicate past gallery and auction sales. Sales by a major gallery, like Gagosian, add to the importance of the art. I also looked at the ownership history of the works, the provenance.

I was looking for background on how the artist fit within his time and a list of museums in which the artist is in the permanent collection. Both of these artists were important.

Lesieur is in the Metropolitan Museum of New York and museums of modern art all over the world, but not in MoMA or other major New York museums. Ippolito is in the Met, MoMA and the Whitney. The art historian, Kenneth Lindsay, wrote in Ippolito's 1975 Binghamton University Gallery retrospective catalog, "He plays out life like a good jazz musician... and improvises a chorus within acknowledged limits of form."

I also read the condition reports on each piece. Condition is critical.

You don't want something in your collection that is damaged.

Most of the auction houses do a good job in reporting condition. If a condition report is not available online, the auction house will provide it to you free upon request.

It is important to start your art search in any auction as early as possible. Research takes time. You need to sort out your interest in works and choose among them.

If there are issues about condition, you need time to examine the work and determine if you can resolve the problems. You must consider and adopt your bidding strategy (a whole chapter later on) and register to bid. So, look at a catalog promptly, whether it is online or in print.

The image on the internet, in my judgement, has improved greatly and produces reliable colors. I expand the image of each work and looked closely at it, with inch by inch magnification if possible, paying particular attention to areas where there are condition issues. Sometimes I do not think condition issues, such as minor cracks at the edge of the painting, make the work unacceptable. Sometimes the issue can be corrected. More about condition and restoration later.

Then I undertook the most important step in my research. I asked my wife, Anne. If we can't agree on a piece, I don't bid. Sometimes, if I am haunted by a piece that she has passed on, I will come back to her and argue my case with more research on the artist and the importance of the work. If it is a woman artist, for example, like any good recovering lawyer, I might push that. But I will never buy if she says no.

She liked the Lesieur and both Ippolitos. After looking closely at each of them in a larger size (you can expand the lot image), she favored the Ippolitos. We discussed both of the paintings by Ippolito and decided on the first (the larger piece), but agreed that if we didn't get the first, we would bid on the second.

It was time to research the artist's past prices. I look for both price and trend. The more recent the better. The more sales the more reliable.

Chapter 3

# THE AUCTION: BIDDING AND SUCCESS

WITH ALL THE BACKGROUND work done, we needed to get ready for the auction itself. If we haven't done business with the auction house before, we had to register and get credit approval by providing a credit card, so allow time for that step. The credit card is only validation. It will not be used. The auction house wants to know you are good for the money if you win a bid. Once you are credit approved, you need only register thereafter for any particular auction and decide your bidding tactics.

There are lots of ways to bid. In this case, we chose the one that was the most fun without being at the auction. We bid on the telephone while watching the auction streaming live on my computer. All auction houses provide a service where they call you when your lot comes up and relay your bid to the auctioneer.

Some auction houses stream audio and video, but Rago only streams audio. All houses stream the numerical bids on screen. You can also bid live, online. But be careful of additional commission charges if you do.

Our lot came around and we were called by the auction house. They were nice and are reliable about transmitting your bid.

In my experience, go to the auction in person if you can. It is the most fun. It is also the most dangerous way to participate. You can sense the atmosphere, feel the emotions and evaluate other bidders. Being among other buyers can get your competitive juices going. Sometimes liking or disliking another buyer by sight can influence your bidding.

I just read a piece in the *Wall Street Journal* about a man who paid

$410,000 for a Delaware car with a license plate numbered 20. People collect low number license plates. The car was worth $10,000. The buyer said his greatest joy was looking across at his competitor and crushing him. That tends to be an expensive pastime.

Being at an auction is the easiest way to break down your bidding discipline. Believe me, I know. My bidding discipline has deserted me at live auctions. If I am lucky, either someone is dumber than I am or, at a certain bidding level, even my discipline reasserts itself, probably because the vision of abject poverty causes hunger pangs.

Rago is in New Jersey. There was no way we were going to New Jersey. I understand there are parts of it that are very nice, but still. Perhaps if we had been thinking of a $100,000 art work at a major New York auction house, we might have gone. (I do think of those paintings from time to time, or even more valuable ones, but then I wake up.)

Bidding strategy is easy. Knock out the other bidders. Bidding tactics are not. The tempo of your bids can communicate information to other bidders, such as determination or a deeper pocket.

We asked our phone representative to bid aggressively from the opening bid (which was well below the low estimate) and not to come back to us until she reached the high estimate, which, in the case of the first Ippolito, was $1,800. We wanted other bidders to believe we would overpay (or leave them hanging out) if they kept bidding.

It takes only two determined people to drive a price to the stratosphere. Several of the prior lots had gone way beyond the high estimate. A Lenore Tawney (1907-2007) multimedia box that I liked had a high estimate of $6,000. It sold for $25,000.

There were three bidders on the Ippolito. The bids quickly escalated to the maximum estimate. We were the under-bidder. The maximum estimate is an important psychological point. No one wants to pay more than retail. But estimates are just an educated guess.

Our auction lady came back to us and we instructed her to go as high as $2,400 and stop. We were willing to spend $3,000 on the piece (it was an oil canvas and a decent size; that is $2,400 plus a 25% commission), but no more. Our next bid was $1,900. It was the winning bid. The whole sequence of events took place in less than two minutes.

Chapter 4

## WHAT IS GREAT ART?

I AM CERTAIN THE BEST way to collect great art on a shoestring is to be at the center of a major art movement, such as Minimalism, to have great taste and access and to pick the right artists. Think of Gertrude Stein in Paris in the early 1900s among the great modern artists. Unfortunately, that doesn't make me think of us.

More to the point, think of Dorothy and Herbert Vogel. She was a librarian. He was a postal worker. They lived in a one-bedroom rent-controlled apartment in New York City. They scrimped and saved to buy art.

The first piece of art they bought was a crushed-metal sculpture by John Chamberlain. They collected over 5,000 works of art in their lifetimes and became embedded and beloved collectors of Minimalism, the austere art movement that followed the exuberance of Abstract Expressionism.

They kept all the art in their small apartment; in the closets, in the bedroom, even in the oven. They could hardly move.

Young artists were their friends, long before those artists became famous. Artists would vie to be in their collection. It added luster to the artist's name. The couple was welcomed everywhere.

In their old age, the Vogels donated their entire collection to the National Gallery in Washington, D.C. It was worth many millions of dollars (and they cleaned out their apartment). The Director of the National Gallery observed that "the radical expansion of intellectual and stylistic expressions . . . since the 1960's [sic] is reflected in the diversity (the)... Vogels collected."

These humble folk became so important, a documentary was made about them. The National Gallery granted them a life annuity in recognition of their generosity, so they could live a more comfortable old age. Instead, they started a new collection.

That isn't me. I know because I was around the Southern California art scene in the '60s. If I had had any money, which I didn't, I would have chosen the wrong artists. I never would have bought that Ed Ruscha oil for $20,000, which would be worth $1,000,000 now.

I wouldn't have chosen well, even if the artists were anointed by L.A. Louvre, the preeminent gallery of the era in Los Angeles. But lots of the artists who were represented by the L.A. Louvre at that time can now be purchased for less than they sold for then. And those are fine artists. The gallery was and is very discriminating.

That is the point of this book.

Artists, in many ways, are like rock stars. A few become internationally celebrated. Many of those deserve it. Maybe they created a new movement or a unique expression of that movement. But, like purchasing branded luxury goods, you are paying a big premium for the name. In the tens of millions of dollars.

Beyond the 20 superstars of a generation, there are 100 or more great artists whose works are wonderful and can bring you joy every day.

By "great," I don't mean an undiscovered artist who will become internationally famous. Or discovering a lost masterpiece. If I did, I would be cruising on a magnificent yacht in the Mediterranean instead of writing this book. I am referring to wonderful artists who produced strong work that you will love to own, and who's work you can afford.

The art market is layered and biased. A Rothko can cost $80,000,000. Probably worth it if you have that kind of money. Broadly speaking, the next level of artists cost millions, but fewer millions. Then, perhaps, the market falls into the hundreds of thousands and finally into the twenty-thousand-dollar range.

But there are a host of artists, collected by major museums all over the world, who produced solid work and who are neglected or bypassed. Most artists are forgotten. These artists sell for thousands of dollars, not tens of thousands.

And you can purchase unique works, not prints. No one, even an art professional, knows the vast majority of dead artists, even if they were admired during their lives. There are just too many.

Art is not necessary. It is a luxury good and an acquired taste. My interest in art, fine food and wine arose after I had achieved some limited success and a bit of money.

I met interesting, accomplished people. Knowledge of food, wine and art were enriching. And it impressed women. But art had it hands down over food and wine. It wasn't fattening!

How do you find these artists? How do you buy their works?

How do you avoid mistakes? How do you have fun, live with beauty and embrace one of the most stimulating and emotionally satisfying things you can do? On a shoestring?

Chapter 5

# WHAT IS A SHOESTRING?

So, what is a shoestring? You may have lace-up boots. I have deck shoes. Anne has high heels.

We have friends who own multi-million-dollar pieces of art, and friends who have collected great prints and multiples. We don't have the wealth to collect million-dollar pieces and we have found that we get more joy from the diversity, variety and textures of unique art works. They are more deeply satisfying to us.

A single painting can easily cost $1,000,000 (or $20,000,000 for that matter). For us, when a picture costs more than $20,000, we get queasy. Our entire collection is worth less than a single piece of branded art (which will be discussed in a later chapter).

And we have several strong pieces that cost less than $5,000. Some cost less than $2,000. That's a shoestring.

Since 2009, when Anne and I started collecting Post-War Art, we made a few lucky acquisitions. We acquired two Dan Christensen (1942-2007) acrylics on paper for about $2,000 each and a wonderful Alice Baber (1928-1982) oil on canvas for the same amount. Baber and Christensen are both lyrical abstract expressionists. The Christensen works were painted in 1979 and the Baber was done in 1962.

Dan Christensen died at the age of 64. Lots of artists seem to die young. He was concerned with the process of painting and the interaction of colors. He began using spray guns and squeegees in his experimentation with painting. His work is in the collections of MoMA and the Whitney.

Alice Baber was married to and divorced from Paul Jenkins, another well-known painter. She painted in the '60s and '70s. Her paintings radiantly fuse light and color by means of ovoid or egg shapes, seeming to float in limitless space.

Although Baber achieved international recognition during the '70s, the curator of her exhibit at the Los Angeles County Museum of Art believed that Baber did not become as well-known as other exponents of stain painting, such as Helen Frankenthaler and Morris Lewis, because she died so young. She died at 54. Baber's art is in the permanent collections of the Guggenheim, the Met, MoMA and the Whitney.

I believed these purchases were flukes. They were rare finds. But I wasn't seeing the bigger picture. I was not conscious at that time of how many artists are forgotten.

It wasn't until the Rago auction, where I found so many great works, that it dawned on me. Now, I believe, it is possible systematically to build a collection of great works in that price range.

Let me give you an example. We recently purchased a 4-foot by 5-foot acrylic and graphite painting on paper by Sonia Gechtoff (1926-2018) for $1,350 plus a 25% commission (we will talk about works on paper as opposed to works on canvas). We loved the piece. In future chapters, I'll speak to how we go about selecting a piece to bid on, but Gechtoff was an important artist in the '70s. *The New York Times*, in 1976, called her "one of the most gifted artists of her generation."

Her work is in many major museum collections, including those of MoMA, the Met and the Guggenheim. She has been included in art magazine articles discussing the most important women painters of her generation. The bibliography of books and articles discussing her work is extensive.

---

Female Abstract Expressionist painters were ignored and largely diminished by their male colleagues and by dealers and curators. It did not help that Gechtoff was a tough, straight-talking, swearing woman who was, in her own words, a feminist before the feminists came along.

The art world may have been more meritocratic in the rest of the country, but New York was the center of Abstract Expressionist art and that was where the money was. Gechtoff moved to New York from San Francisco and did important work there. She was promptly forgotten.

Of course, the $1,350 plus the 25% commission was only the beginning and there is another chapter on the out-the-door cost of a painting before you get it on your wall. But, you get the point.

Here is a wonderful, large piece of art, by a first-class artist of whom you never heard, nor had we, that we want to live with. All for the price of a soppy, mass-produced oil we could buy at the local furniture store or a small lithograph in an edition of 250 copies by an internationally famous artist.

My shoestring is not yours. But even with an annual budget of $10,000 (which I know is a lot of money), you can acquire several strong pieces if you are careful. And you will start on a fascinating avocation where you will learn, be entertained and experience joy.

The art world is, indeed, just that. If you go through the pinhole, there is a whole universe. A different language, different people and different experiences. It is an adventure that can give you a lifetime of pleasure.

As the Chinese say, the journey of a thousand miles begins with a single step.

## Chapter 6

## DEAD ARTISTS

THE REASON I COLLECT dead artists is because I like people. The artists I have known can be charming (or total jerks) and interesting. They may be suffering economically. And I care.

I don't want to be influenced by my emotions, at least not for the artists. I feel I can be more objective about artists whose work is done, where my strengths in analysis, research and finance give me an edge.

In any business dealing I have always sought an edge by finding out-of-the-way opportunities and bringing to bear my skills and experience. I refer to it as my "funeral home theory of business." No one wants to be an undertaker, but some people have made it very profitable for generations. The same theory applies to collecting art.

I fear that among living artists, I don't know enough about art trends throughout the world, what is evolving or what new ideas are taking shape. In some circles, abstract painting is being rejected for figurative expression. Will this be an important direction?

I have enough experience to know that going by what I like (and I think I may have a pretty good eye) is not enough. I can easily love something that will be irrelevant.

And collecting contemporary art by living artists can be expensive. Considerably more expensive than the level at which I am comfortable collecting. Have you ever been to a gallery opening where a decent sized unique work by an established contemporary artist is priced at $2,000 or even $5,000?

I can understand, but not interpret, the pricing of contemporary art. There are too many influences that do not have to do with quality and value. In the documentary *The Price of Everything*, the internationally famous artist Gerhard Richter looks at a small, scraped canvas painting he created and said, "This is the value of a house. I like it, but it is not a house."

I am more comfortable where the quality and quantity of an artist's work is complete. The artist is dead. There will be no more. All the facts are established. Where I can research the artist's importance and influence.

There were a lot of wonderful artists, particularly women, who never had a strong following. Then, most were forgotten.

Women and Black artists are stirring more and more interest. In July, 2018, *The New York Times* observed that many top collectors have added women and Black artists to their shopping lists. The attention was inspired by museum curators' desire to rehabilitate marginalized and neglected talent. The Met has recently mounted a major retrospective of an underappreciated Black artist, Kerry James Marshall (b. 1955) and his life-long effort to make an invisible American Black culture visible.

*ARTnews*, in September 2018, quoted Mark Payot, a partner in Hauser & Wirth, a major gallery, on the historical lack of mainstream attention to Black artists. "From a dealer's point of view, there is a great opportunity—and not because they are African-American, but because they are great artists." Despite the headlines of records-setting auction prices for a few Black artists, the reappraisal has just begun. Payot continued, "Yes, we are moving in the right direction but, take out the top segment, and progress is much less than people think."

What is next? I don't know, but if you collect living artists and want great art, you have to get ahead of the curve, and seek to exploit the trends. Or you can avoid second-guessing the trends entirely and search in the attic of art.

The decade of the 1960s offers some unique opportunities in abstract art. Only a few great Abstract Expressionists got all the attention. There are numerous, extraordinary artists who were shoved to the back, particularly women, Blacks and both women and men from Latin America.

Most artists do not have a lot of loyal collectors. If two do not show up at a particular auction, less demand results in lower prices.

For example, Ray Johnson (1927-1995) was an artist classed with the great Pop artists, such as Roy Lichtenstein, Andy Warhol and Claus Oldenburg. In fact, those artists were collectors of his work. Indeed, they were among his few collectors.

Johnson was and is almost unknown to the public. A man to whom relationships did not come easily. He wasn't socially adept and he became a recluse after he fled New York in 1967.

Johnson did not seek gallery representation and submitted to it only grudgingly. No one knew what work he was doing. He dropped from sight after he moved from New York, and from memory after his suicide in 1995. His work does not come at auction frequently. Auction houses may have been reluctant to try and sell his work. When they do, the low price of his work, in relation to his peers, reflects the demand.

The chances of making money in collecting forgotten artists, or even recouping your purchase price, are not good. Taking advantage of the market's pricing peculiarities cuts both ways.

If there is no demand now for a forgotten artist, there is no reason to believe there will be demand when you choose to sell. Coupled with the 25% commission on both purchase and sale, the chances are remote, but not impossible.

Art is about passion, not money, as every collector knows. Barney Ebsworth, a noted collector, looking back on the incredible artworks he had lived with, said, "It is the emotional and intellectual experience of collecting that has been the most glorious and rewarding aspect of my life."

We love having a home filled with art. It makes me happy every time I walk through our house. And when I walk out the door, the feeling doesn't go away.

## Chapter 7

## INSECURITY

INSECURITY IS RAMPANT AMONG art collectors. And with good reason. All collectors fear being made to play the fool. To be humiliated among people they had hoped to impress.

There are lots of ways to be misled. In the areas of Old Masters and Abstract Expressionism, there are forgeries. Particularly in pre-war Modern Art, there is also the question of provenance, a record of ownership. The work might be Nazi war loot and subject to questions of title.

In ancient works there may be claims to title by the homeland. And later copies, in addition to forgery, become an issue. The Roman's made excellent copies of ancient Greek statues.

In foreign countries, there may be artists' rights that add to the cost of the piece or that may limit reproduction in catalogs or magazines. In contemporary art, it is always the question of what is it and will it be important?

There were even fraud cases where provenance and forgery came together. When John Drewe met John Myatt, Myatt's life was a shambles. He was desperate for money. Myatt was a competent forger, although he painted with materials that were not used by the artists he forged.

But the heart of the scam, the thing that set the art world on its ear, was the creation of provenance that John Drewe devised. A seemingly proper Englishman who represented himself as a collector and art scholar, he applied to do research in the archives of London's Tate and the Victoria and Albert's National Art Library. He gave himself as a reference, using a false name.

Drewe seeded the museums' records with fake documents, cards and letters. He even altered a 1955 exhibition catalog from a defunct gallery to insert pictures and descriptions of Myatt's forgeries of Giacometti, Dubuffet and Chagall.

There were so many false documents and so many fabricated records, spread across so many artists, that neither the Tate nor the Victoria and Albert may ever know the extent of the corruption of their records. Only 73 of Myatt's 200 paintings have been located by the police. Interestingly, Myatt became something of a folk hero and after leaving prison had a thriving career selling his "genuine fakes."

---

Of course, there is the basic need to be able to tell a strong work of art from one that is mediocre or just bad. Oh yes, major artists, indeed every artist, has produced bad work. Everyone has Monday mornings.

Or the worst fears. Did you just stupidly pay too much? Did you buy something insignificant? Even dumb?

Looking back, Cubism seems obvious. Dada is startling but difficult to comprehend. Each of these was despised by the art world at first. Many art movements still are, some with very good reason. In the words of a lawyer I once called for a reference on a possible legal hire, "He is a was if he ever was an is." You need to be smart enough to tell the "is." I'm not.

It is easy in hindsight and incredibly hard in prospect to know what is going on all over the art world. And you need to know before you can address the question of what will be important or lasting.

I had the same problem with venture capital investing in tech companies. How did I know that the company seeking money to develop software to computerize doctor's records did not have a product that was less effective, or was made obsolete by software being developed in a garage in Sweden? I couldn't see the whole picture, even if I knew that what I was looking at was a great product. It all made me crazy and insecure. Of course, if you had enough money, you could purchase a share of a number of companies and hope that one would be a home run. I don't have enough money.

Auctions, by definition, represent the fair market value of a work of art at the moment of sale. (Maybe. There have been a few examples of works selling for significantly more than similar works available in galleries within a mile. That relates more to the people's knowledge and bidding discipline than to the market.) But this moment may not be tomorrow's fair market value.

You can go to a lot of gallery openings. The world of living artists is exciting. You get to know artists and dealers. You meet interesting people. And you get to drink a lot of bad wine. But you can never go to enough openings. Even if you visit all the galleries in New York every week, there are other galleries in London, Berlin and Tokyo.

And galleries don't do much to help you with pricing. Galleries are less pressured by current trends, so they are slower to lower prices on their inventory. A collector coming in who likes a piece is less likely to do the price research and even if he or she does, is less likely to be willing to wait for another piece by the same artist to come up at auction. That is, unless the price is glaringly out of line. I saw a nice Robert Natkin in a gallery. The owner was asking $25,000. That was about three times the auction value. I know. I bought a better one.

I am frugal as well as insecure. I also don't have a lot of money. I have a value equation in my head with which I have to live. I am often wrong, but never uncertain. I need to have room to make mistakes.

We could hire an art advisor. They study the market and spend all their time listening and perhaps, even thinking. Advisors provide a counter-balance to the self-interest that pervades each aspect of the art world (including the advisors themselves, unless you employ them on a retainer, not a commission.) Someone to hold a hand. There are some good ones. They are expensive.

We can't afford an art advisor. We had to find a way to do it ourselves. We needed to find a way to maximize our education and minimize our insecurities on a small budget.

# Chapter 8
## ABOUT US

IT MAY BE USEFUL to know something of our background. I started collecting art before I married Anne. I have been collecting art for more than 35 years.

Our collection is anchored in Post-War abstract art, created during the 1970s. Almost all of the work is one-of-a kind-pieces (which, again, I refer to as uniques, to distinguish them from prints), with about half on paper and half on canvas or some other surface, such as a board.

I took a bachelor's degree in accounting with a minor in economics. I got an M.B.A. before trundling off to law school at Harvard. During my 37 years of practice, I bought and sold large companies, not art. I am a financial guy.

I have written three art world mysteries as well as two other novels and I am a published poet. Who knew? No one is more surprised at my creative side than I am.

Anne has a degree in industrial design and journalism and is the author or editor of three books. She still works as a media consultant.

We are both avid collectors. She loves art as much as I do, but I take the lead in identifying the works from which we choose. One honey-do I enjoy.

For the first 40 years of my life, I had no inkling about art. I think I took an art appreciation course in college. I was a committed reader, but I had yet to discover wine and food, much less my own creative talents.

But I have a curious mind. It made me a good lawyer. I want to know how things work, and why. I learned to apply methods and knowledge from one area to another; to think laterally.

One day, a long time ago, I started thinking about the art market. Not art, but the market for art. It wasn't apparent to me why a Van Gogh was worth $2,000,000 (okay, it was a really long time ago) and another painting was worth $100,000. They both looked great to me. I figured if I could solve this conundrum, I could get rich. I failed on both counts.

But I spent the next three years reading about art. It was fascinating. I didn't have the money to buy anything, but I was hooked. I started going to galleries and looking at street art.

I bought my first piece of art in 1983, a large oil by Arnold Mesches (1923-2016). It made me feel terrific. It cost $8,500 and the gallery gave me a year to pay it off. I got to meet Arnold.

The painting was a diptych with a re-rendering on one panel of the classical image of Betsy Ross with the American Flag draped across her lap, and a very strong portrait of what might be a Black man, painted in bold curving yellow and black strokes, on the other. It was a strong piece. It was very painterly and the juxtaposing of the images created an intellectual underpinning to the work.

I asked Arnold what the painting meant. I was not very smart about art. He laughed and said he wasn't about to ruin my fun.

I loved the painting for years and eventually gave it to a university museum when I moved. It wouldn't fit into my new house.

If you give a painting to a museum, you get the present market value of the art as a deduction, and you do not have to recognize a capital gain on the transfer. My tax deduction just about equaled what I paid, but what the heck. I wasn't in it for the money.

I started collecting Asian art and antique canes. Then my house in Santa Barbara burned down in the Tea Fire in 2008 and I had to start again.

I wanted to explore a completely different area of art. Anne and I decided to collect contemporary art. We chose works on paper because they were cheaper. I thought that meant mostly prints, not unique pieces, and we acquired some wonderful works. We bought a large, wall-sized Lichtenstein and a smaller Frankenthaler for $22,000 and $9,000 at a local fine arts auction.

We started looking at auctions and having a great time. Then I started thinking about it. We began looking beyond Sotheby's and Christie's and the galleries. We didn't have the money to play with them.

Then we discovered unique pieces existed on paper (other than prints, drawings and watercolors). I found a Rolf Scarlett (1889-1984) gouache and graphite work on paper we liked in a Swann auction. I looked him up. Scarlett has a great many works in the Guggenheim. Why it has so many Scarletts has been the subject of controversy. The first director, a woman, was his patron and perhaps was more.

But there it was. If we looked hard enough, we could find unique art we could afford. Maybe there were others. So, our search began.

Some people concentrate on artists they like and buy several works by them. They become friends with the artists. They enter their lives. That isn't me. I do not want to have several pieces by the same artist.

The only exception in our collection are 3 works by Dan Christensen, all from the same series. All three are uniques, done in 1979-1980. Two are acrylic on paper while the third is acrylic on untreated canvas.

They are very subtle and diverge from my love of bright colors and definition. So subtle in fact that we almost didn't buy them, they looked so bland in the catalog. We seem to have always tended toward hard-edge abstract art although there are now many paintings in our collection that are boldly colored, but more fluid.

All three of the Christensens hang in our master bedroom, a prime location. I love them. Vivid colors peek through a bland over-wash. And the works are textured so that a line is thickened and raised or the same color is mopped on in one place and painted on smoothly below. In any case, they are objects to me of sheer admiration and it thrills me to look at them closely.

# Chapter 9

## WHERE TO LOOK

BEFORE OUR HOUSE BURNED down in a California wildfire, I had collected Oriental art and antique Oriental canes for years. While it was heart-breaking to lose such wonderful art on my watch, the timing of the fire was fortuitous because I had reached a point of saturation with my areas of collecting.

As with all collections, it evolved. Sometimes, evolution is forced by circumstances outside your control. Sometimes it comes about as you gain more knowledge, your taste matures or your financial circumstances change, temporarily or permanently.

At our first auction after the fire, a local auction in Santa Monica, we bought several prints by internationally famous artists, like Lichtenstein and Frankenthaler, plus a few oil paintings by artists I didn't know, but whose work we liked. By chance, most of the work was created between the mid-70s to mid-80s and that period became the center of our collection.

Like most people at the start, we were trying to buy art to fill the walls of our new home, although we knew we wanted to form a collection. I had told our architect that we wanted our new house to speak of art. (That means we wanted walls and light.)

Then I got interested and started to study. First, I found that works on paper were much broader than just prints. I knew about watercolor and drawings, of course, although I hadn't thought of them. But there were also gouache and acrylic works. In fact, there were all kinds of unique works on paper. And works on paper are usually cheaper than works on canvas. I could have unique works by great artists I might be able to afford.

Since I did not have a lot of money to spend after that first rush of insurance funds, I looked for ways I could acquire art we liked and wanted, for prices in our range.

I loved looking at the work offered at the major auction houses in their evening sales, but $5 million dollars was a bit out of our league. So, I looked at their day auctions. That didn't work. The prices were often in the hundreds of thousands of dollars. At that time, our budget was a total of about $20,000 or $30,000 a year.

Christie's had introduced the First Open internet-only auctions. It was Christie's announced purpose to offer good art at reasonable prices to interest first time collectors. While I wasn't a first-time collector, I had the budget of one. I think we acquired a couple of pieces from Christie's.

Sotheby's had online auctions of lower priced works where no buyer's premium was added to the hammer price. In other words, the price was not increased by a 25% commission. While these auctions were small potato prices in the auction world, they were still too expensive for me. The "no commission" gambit created more demand. It seemed to drive up the price even more than the 25% savings. But it was fun to look.

I have an inquisitive mind, so I started exploring more off-beat auctions. I looked at Doyle's Art+Design auction. Bonham's had a similar auction that combined furniture with fine art. I thought it was an unusual dilution of the fine art, and I thought there would be less likelihood these auctions would attract other bidders. We acquired several pieces that we loved, in the $5,000 to $10,000 range. We were getting there.

We went down to the Los Angeles Modern auction in Van Nuys, California. It was a kick to be at a live auction again. They had some really good works (I bought an Ed Moses unique work on paper at three times the estimate in a great display of lack of discipline. Fortunately, the tab was "only" $12,000, all in.)

But they had several abstract artists from the California Hard-Edge movement, so called because of their discipline (which I could learn from) in the use of line and color. And a lot of other quality work, including a small Calder mobile that sold for $800,000. Plus, we got free ice cream.

Last year was a tough year. Our $5,000 total budget set some new constraints and sent me off in a new direction. And that, in turn, led to some great discoveries.

It was by sheer chance I discovered Bidsquare, the auction house aggregator. These smaller, local auction houses listed on Bidsquare offered some really good art (and some really awful art, too). The sale of art on the internet has exploded. There now are numerous buying sites and online auctions. But the development of auction aggregators proved particularly important to us.

Until then, art fairs had been the great trend in the art world. They are to galleries as aggregators are to auction houses, but in a physical way. Art fairs, like Art Basel in Switzerland, which have blossomed all over the world, are temporary giant supermarkets of art. They allow the galleries who purchase booths to reach large numbers of new people, but extract heavy costs in booth fees, shipping and travel.

There were 55 art fairs throughout the world in 2000. Now there are 260. Dealers report that 46% of their sales are made at art fairs. The stronger galleries are finding new buyers and growing stronger.

While these fairs are convenient for the collector and often worth a gallery's effort and expense, they put smaller galleries at a competitive disadvantage. Galleries are closing their doors because of higher rents at home, fees levied by the art fairs, but more importantly because bigger galleries are poaching young artistic talent before they can generate profit for the smaller galleries. Art fairs have turned the brick and mortar gallery business on its ear and dramatically changed its economics. But the market is still evolving in ways both advantageous to art fairs and threatening to them.

The internet has revolutionized the auction world, but it has had an even broader impact on the business of art. Instagram has changed the face of art marketing. It has become the most powerful marketing instrument of art sales. Everyone in art marketing has an Instagram account. It has hit the sweet spot in the sharing of art information.

Branded dealers use Instagram to pre-sell art destined for art fairs. But Instagram is also creating a challenge to the art fairs. It may be the catalyst to wean out smaller, less successful fairs, even absent an economic slow-down. The growth of art fairs has been exponential. Professionals say fairs have reached the saturation point. How many fairs can a collector attend?

And they are expensive for dealers, particularly because many fairs require dealers to maintain a physical gallery space as a condition to participation, further squeezing the resources of mid-level galleries. Some have resolved to give up fairs entirely and use Instagram to reach the national and international market to promote their programs. It is a function only art fairs could perform previously.

There are instances where dealers have made sales for tens of thousands of dollars directly over Instagram. Anders Petterson, the author of the Hiscox Online Art Trade report said "Instagram has become the leading social media tool for discovering, showing and following art, particularly for people below the age of 35." Collectors can choose eye-grabbing pieces of art while strolling through the endless gallery of the internet. Instagram has been called the pusher that feeds the addiction of the art collector.

On January 16, 2019, Ben Davis announced, *in ARTnews,* that he had seen the future in an ordinary brown, speckled egg. He was referring to the image on Instagram that in 10 days attracted 42 million viewers. He observed that the egg seemed to represent a powerful anti-aesthetic current at play. That the same forces that gave rise to the artificiality of the Instagram experience had also given birth to something like an intuitive people's conceptualism. "You could definitely say that a world where an ordinary egg is our biggest star is a world where the distinction between life and art has become totally scrambled."

The inflection point caused in the art world by the internet has only begun to become apparent. However, in the auction market, the internet has already benefited collectors with a limited budget. It has increased supply and demand has not yet caught up. Bidsquare and Invaluable, the auction house aggregators, have proven particularly valuable in the price range I wanted to buy and the artists in which I was interested. They permit local auction houses to market their art auctions more widely, online. I would never have run across them otherwise. They are often located in small cities or the suburbs. They offer more underappreciated or forgotten artists than I have found anywhere else and their price points are intriguing.

In our area of Post-War abstract art, I found two houses that seem special, Rago Auctions, that I mentioned before, and L.H. Hindman. I am sure I will find others.

The aggregators present a lot of auction houses that are irrelevant to me. So, I waste time looking at auctions that hold no interest for me, either because of the quality of the works they are selling, or because I feel compelled to make sure there isn't a treasure in the poop.

But we have been pleased with the pieces we have purchased. The condition was as presented. We acquired both the Sonia Gechtoff acrylic on paper and the Angelo Ippolito work on canvas from Rago, both wonderful artists widely collected by important museums.

We bought these pieces because we loved them and we wanted them in our collection. It was not a matter of price. Both pieces are strong works. And all-in, we stayed within our $5,000 budget for both.

These were not just flukes. There were half a dozen pieces in the Rago auction Anne and I considered. They were really good. There were many more than six we disqualified for other reasons. It was hard to decide what we wanted to bid on. And that does not consider those pieces that were too large to fit our wall space or were a little more than we could afford this year.

I recommended pieces we weren't going to bid on to friends, including a wonderful William Tillyer water color in the L.H. Hindman auction. I must admit, I was tempted by the Tillyer. As Oscar Wilde said, "I can resist anything but temptation." I really loved it.

I looked at it several times over the weeks before the auction. Fortunately, it was too big to fit any wall we had available and there was no existing piece in our collection we wanted to sell to make space for it.

It will be frustrating to look at a lot of auctions before you are ready to buy because you will feel you are missing all the great deals. You aren't. There are always more auctions and more great art. Like any matter of taste, it takes a while and can only be honed by experience and study.

Chapter 10

# THE ESSENTIALS

THERE ARE MANY TYPES of fine art. Painting, sculpture, prints, drawings, conceptual art, performance art and computer art, to name a few. This book focuses on paintings, but let's look at the others briefly.

Sculpture may be carved or molded from any material; stone, marble, wood or plaster, among others. Michelangelo's *David* is a magnificent example of marble sculpture. Michelangelo made a profound statement about art. He said the sculpture he saw was inside the stone, and he only had to remove the excess pieces.

What I think he meant is that if you are an artist, the work comes whole to you in your mind. I find that to be true in many endeavors. I believe a fine carpenter can see in his mind how the pieces fit together. I know I cannot.

An author can see the whole book, although he may need to repeat the process to create each chapter. Mozart said he could hear an entire piece of music in his mind. He just had to write it down.

The *David*, by its nature, is a one-of-a-kind piece of sculpture. It was carved out of marble. Bronze sculpture is different.

A bronze piece is usually cast multiple times from the same mold. The sculptor makes a model for the mold or the mold itself, then delivers it to a foundry to be cast. Casts are sometimes made during the artist's life and are sometimes cast after his death. Rodin's sculptures were cast both before and after his death, within the limits of the edition. An edition is the number of replications, set by the artist. The value of a pre-death cast and post-death cast is different. Use care.

Prints are really people's art. The artist makes a plate, using one of several methods, including carving into the plate or cutting into it.

But beware. The art world is a colorful and dangerous place. There are a lot of people who want to take your money in a lot of ways. There was a notorious scam involving Salvador Dali. Dali needed money. He signed whole piles of blank sheets of paper and sold them.

The buyers bought rights to Dali images and reproduced them on the signed sheets. They sold the works as original, signed prints for a lot of money. But Dali did not supervise or approve the prints. They were signed beforehand.

So, anyone buying a Dali print has to be careful. The scandal caused turmoil in the market when it was discovered. The market for Dali prints has not recovered.

At some point, you will be tempted to buy a piece of art by an artist you know and love because the piece is such a bargain. You will work hard to convince yourself you like it.

Mira Rubell, a well-known collector, said "How do you know when you need to acquire a piece? How do you know you are in love? If you listen to your emotions, you know." And like knowing you are in love, sometimes you're wrong.

Don't invite someone into your home you don't love. The piece will be irritating. If you don't love it at the outset, you won't grow to love it by seeing it daily on your wall. I have done it. It is one of the strongest confirmations that art is about passion, not money.

This doesn't apply to an artwork that intrigues you. One that is, perhaps, less accessible. A piece like that is a worthy addition to your collection. You may grow to love it or hate it, but you will grow. This interaction is part of the great privilege of owning art.

Presence in a museum's permanent collection tend to validate the importance of an artist. The more museums, the greater the validation. The more important the museum, the greater the validation.

Is the artist in the top museums like Museum of Modern Art (MoMA), the Whitney or the Guggenheim in New York? (The Metropolitan Museum of Art doesn't specialize in Post-War and Contemporary Art. It is less likely they will have collected a neglected artist.)

Then there are the other great museums throughout the country. The Los Angeles County Museum of Art and MOCA, the Art Institute of Chicago, the Philadelphia Museum of Art, the Hirschhorn and the San Francisco Museum of Modern Art to name a very few outside of New York.

These collections are important reference points. The more major museums an artist is in, the more likely the importance of the artist. A curator must have thought the artist was important enough to present the work to their Collections Committee. And the Collections Committee must have felt the artist's position warranted acceptance of the donation of the work or its acquisition. The Collections Committee generally consists of senior museum staff and trustees.

Museums do not accept art donations casually. That may surprise you. After all, isn't it a gift? It costs them nothing. Wrong.

It doesn't matter how much a donated picture is worth (unless it is a really big number). Once the work enters the museum collection, it becomes a financial liability, not an asset (I know it is worth money, but if the money cannot be realized, that is not an asset.) The art must be stored, insured, secured, conserved and curated, all of which cost money.

Selling the art is very difficult for a museum and fraught with public relations problems. No museum undertakes deaccessioning lightly or often. And the use of the proceeds is restricted, even if the donor has imposed no restrictions. The proceeds must be used to purchase new art, not for operating expenses or additions to the endowment. More liabilities.

The Berkshire Museum in Pittsfield, Massachusetts had been losing $1,000,000 a year for a decade. It was on the verge of financial collapse. The Board was desperate. In July 2017, to keep its doors open, they voted to sell 40 pieces of art, including Norman Rockwell's *Shuffleton's Barbershop*.

A firestorm ensued. Critics and museum associations objected vehemently, saying that art should not be treated as a commodity. A judge blocked the sale at the request of the Attorney General. A seven-month investigation ensued. Judge David Lowy, of the

Massachusetts Supreme Judicial Court, in his decision, acknowledged the serious concerns of some, but found that the museum had demonstrated that selling the works was vital to its survival.

The Association of Art Museum Directors, one of the major museum organizations, citing the use of the proceeds for other than art acquisition, sanctioned the Berkshire Museum and asked each of their 243 members to refrain from collaborating with the Berkshire Museum and to not lend to it or borrow works of art from it. The museum's executive director resigned with the gratitude of the Board for leading it through such a challenging time.

Unless the art work is believed to be important to the museum's collection, the museum will pass on accepting proffered gifts. It doesn't happen often because the curator is the gatekeeper, so many proposed gifts of art don't even get that far. It is crushing for a curator to present an art work and have it turned down by the Collections Committee. The more important the museum, the less likely they are to accept a donation.

The "permanent collection" reference is important. There are other collections maintained by museums. For instance, the museum may maintain a study collection of objects outside of the permanent collection. Most works owned by a museum are in their permanent collection. Assume the art work is, but have just a hint of suspicion.

Research is the key to collecting, particularly in collecting great art on a shoestring. The internet has become an invaluable resource in art research. You also might consider subscribing to *ARTnews* or *ArtForum* magazine or one of the art newsletters. You can keep up with what is happening in the art world. And perhaps get some ideas.

The provenance (history of ownership) is important for several reasons. You want to ascertain that the painting is real, not a forgery or a copy and that the seller has good title.

Christie's was just sued by a buyer, who, a decade ago, purchased a Sisley oil for several hundred thousand dollars. A third party claimed the work was looted by the Nazis and the seller did not have good title. This true owner was now seeking return of the art from Christie's buyer. Christie's claimed it was not negligent in its examination of the provenance of the art and it could not have reasonably discovered that the art had been looted.

More importantly, at least on the level Anne and I collect, if the provenance discloses that the piece has passed through the hands of a major gallery, we can be certain, at least at that time, the artist was well regarded. If the piece was previously sold at auction, we can ascertain the price the piece was sold for and the time it remained in the hands of the buyer. If it was resold quickly, it raises a concern that there is something wrong with the work. There need not be. But it raises a red flag.

# Chapter II

## LOOK FOR THE EDGE

To collect great art on a shoestring, you need to look for an edge over other buyers. Maybe you are better at research or know more about the artist. Maybe you collect art in areas or periods in which others are not interested or artists who are unknown to others. Or you look in places others don't look. The more you reduce competition, the lower the price. Simple supply and demand.

Select a few artists you would like to collect. In doing so, you have an important choice. Living artists continue to produce. If they are prolific, it will affect the future price of their works. More supply. If demand for their art does not grow, the price will drop. If their buzz fades, the price will drop.

It is harder to place living artists in the evolution of art. Are they ground breaking? Is their work singular or are there others who are working in the same style? If so, are they the best? The first? Is the movement important? Will they be the standout? How much is one of 200 paintings sprayed on with a fire extinguisher worth?

There is also the issue of fads. A hot painter's price may be sky high. You can be right about the artist, but if more collectors have been right before you, and you are behind the curve, the price may exceed the value. And there are innumerable examples of artists who have been adored and then dumped. Whose price has crashed. Paul Jenkins is an example.

Jenkins made his art by putting paint on a surface, then manipulating the surface. It was a colorful, flowing form of Abstract

Expressionism. He allowed his paintings to evolve almost by chance. His pictures were each called *Phenomena*.

He was a sensation. His art was featured in a movie. He soared. His name was on everyone's lips.

We were having lunch in a friend's garden with their Sotheby's expert in contemporary art, who was visiting. It was one of those wonderful art afternoons. Warm, with a gentle breeze. A natural quiet. Stimulating conversation.

Someone asked about problems in valuing art. His example, out of the blue, was the break in the price of Paul Jenkins' art.

That made me a little uneasy. It was early in our collecting and we had just bought a Paul Jenkins watercolor. I nearly choked on my soup. Fortunately, we had purchased after his price crashed. I knew nothing about Jenkins' rise and fall. It scared the heck out of me.

Let's be ghoulish. It is easier to look back than to prophesize. An artist's place in art is more established. His (or her) importance is reflected in museum collections. And, s/he is more readily forgotten. Most artists are.

Start with women. That is always a good place to start. Before the mid-twentieth century, how many famous female artists can you name? Perhaps Mary Cassatt.

Among the Abstract Expressionists, how many women became the international superstars of the twentieth century? How about one. Maybe two, if you want to count a sculptor. So, was Helen Frankenthaler, who appeared among (well, she evolved from) the Abstract Expressionists, unique? The only great woman artist of the Post-War era?

Well, no. There have been a lot of great women artists in the past. Collected by the major museums. There are wonderful pictures they created that are available for a few thousand dollars. Have you ever heard of Grace Harrington, Jay DeFeo or Judith Godwin? Of course not. Alice Baber? I had never heard of her.

You can go either forwards or backwards in finding artists you want to collect. Forward is identifying the artists from research, then finding examples of their work you love at auction or in a gallery.

Backwards is identifying a piece in an auction that thrills you after a lot of looking, then finding out about the artist. I prefer the latter, with a heavy dollop of the former. Both approaches overlap. It is a question of emphasis.

There are a whole group of women who painted wonderful pictures in the 1960s who are forgotten. It is a great period to explore. Even earlier. Did you know Dora Marr, Picasso's model and mistress, was a good artist? I didn't.

Think about the estuaries of art. If art is a great river, then there are currents and flows. Places where great things are hidden below the surface. Where they get stuck on fallen branches. Like Outsider Art. Research it. Explore.

What about the bad boys? Those who did something to offend the art world? Is that even possible?

Theodoros Stamos managed it. He was an artist and so close to Mark Rothko that Rothko named him one of the executors of his estate. Artists, authors and other creative people often name a separate person to administer their artistic estate, apart from lawyers or banks who handle legal, tax and financial matters.

Stamos and Rothko's financial executor were convicted of cheating the Rothko estate along with Marlborough, Rothko's gallery. Stamos agreed to the scheme because Marlborough offered to represent him if he did so. Stamos didn't even get part of the loot.

The art world was horrified at the betrayal of one of its giants and Stamos was banished. The art world shunned him and his paintings. He moved back to Greece.

But Stamos was a terrific artist. Do you want great art on a shoestring? Does it bother you to have a bad boy hanging on the wall? Even if the work is emotionally involving and intriguing.

Then there are Black artists. I deliberately used the term "Black" and not "African-American" because you should not think only of Americans. Art is international, and always has been.

"The rise of African-American artists is part of a broader tendency to re-evaluate neglected artists that has been going on for years," Candace Worth, an art advisor based in New York, said in March 2018.

"Art history isn't just about the big Ab-Ex guys anymore. . . We're opening a conversation, and the market is playing catch-up." She was referring to the contemporary art phenomenon. The sentiment applies universally, I believe.

Black artists were even less appreciated than women. Sam Gilliam has been appreciated, forgotten, rediscovered and forgotten again. Now he is becoming an overnight success. He paints marvelous pictures.

What about foreign art movements? Latin American art is great. Perhaps Latin American art from the '60s?

Then, there is the forgotten corner of these forgotten artists. These artists represent a more difficult, but rewarding journey. They are mostly older Black artists. They are not collected in all the top museums. They do not have the same vetting.

And now, along with Blacks, Soviet era Hungarian woman are being discovered. Think of them all as not forgotten, but never remembered. More research is required. More study. And you need to be surer of yourself. But they are wonderful.

In the last ten years, Blacks and foreign artists have gotten more praise. But they painted 40 years ago. How many came to the attention of critics and major museums? They sometimes are widely collected, but they are not in MoMA or the Whitney.

Charles Searles died in 2004. He was a Black artist who grew up in Philadelphia. He was also a skilled carpenter. He moved away from painting into vibrantly colored sculpture that seem to dance in space. His work is in the collections of the Smithsonian and the Philadelphia Museum of Art. They are worth your time and effort.

When you get your desired list of artists down to some manageable number, start looking at your artists' work online. See as much as you can find. You want to explore the various periods of their art, since artists keep evolving and get bored or feel they have satisfied their exploration in a series of pieces. You are seeking to understand the development of their work and to understand outliers. These can be one-off experiments or just bad work.

If it turns out you are too late to the game, strike the artist. You are not going to find a unique work by Helen Frankenthaler you can afford. Nor one by Elaine de Kooning. She has been rediscovered. But there are a lot of women artists of her quality who are underappreciated or not even on the radar. You have to delve deeper.

Don't get discouraged. It is difficult to find a really good piece at a really good price. These are treasures. Treasures are rare.

When you find one, you may be disappointed when you are out-bid. It may happen time after time. I lost two pieces in a row just last month. This is hard work, but wonderfully satisfying when you succeed.

If you find a piece and succeed in buying it, it is a terrific feeling. And to own one will give you joy every day for years to come.

The art world has obviously changed in the last forty years. Huge amounts of cash have flowed in. The prices of major pieces of art have soared. They now cost as much as tall buildings. Billionaires vie for perceived masterpieces. The artist Damion Hirst, very much alive, makes millions from his work.

How can we even hope to compete? We can't. Nor, at least in our case, do we want to. We want to burrow among the trees, in the undergrowth, where no one else is looking. All the attention is at the top.

If you want to collect great art on a shoestring, you need to explore the jungle. But remember, it is a jungle.

Chapter 12

# THE JUNGLE: HOW TO SELECT ART

I LOOK AT ART in three steps. A piece of art must touch me emotionally. I consider this the critical step in collecting. Art must first engage my heart. I don't have to love it, but it has to intrigue me.

If it does, I want to understand the intellectual background of the piece. I need to do my research. Much of modern art centers on the intellectual idea underlying the creation of the work.

Marcel Duchamp stood art on its ear when he submitted an upside-down porcelain urinal to a progressive, jury-free New York art exhibition. It was signed "J. Mutt" and entitled *Fountain*. (It was rejected by a horrified board, even though they were bound by the rules of the exhibit to accept it.)

Duchamp professed that taking an ordinary article and placing it so that its useful significance disappeared created a new thought for that object. It was art because he chose it. And he was an artist. The art was in the idea.

This concept has had extraordinary power in twentieth century art, perhaps one of its most powerful. It questioned the very basis of art. I would not have been smart enough to be first in line to buy that piece of art.

Where does a particular piece fit in the great river of art? A work can be influenced by another piece of art or another artist, but shy away from derivative art. Derivative art is similar to another, usually more famous, artist's, style. One of the first pieces I bought many years ago was too close to the style of Chagall. The art paled over time.

When two artists create similar styles at the same time, such as Braque and Picasso, that is parallel development. Like Ellsworth Kelly and Carmen Herrera. It is obviously important to distinguish influence from derivation. It requires research and experience.

Finally, if I am still interested, I want to understand the technical achievement in creating the work. This gets tricky with some contemporary work. How good is the painter? Is he or she technically proficient? Is it important? You'll see.

Is a piece of cord nailed to a board art? You bet. Sometimes.

Like all matters of taste, to determine what you like in art is a matter of experience. Over time, your taste will change. And that's okay. You will make mistakes, but we all do. So, take a while to just look. There will always be another great piece of art for sale.

I love to look at art. Not just in museums. There are so many art catalogs, online auctions, online galleries and sales that you can find innumerable places to just experience art. And you can look for free. In many cases, you can also see the price estimates or what the pieces sold for.

There are books to read. Of course, there are the classic books on art history like you read in college. And there are college extension courses.

But there are many interesting stories of the art world and many genre art books, such as mysteries written by Charlotte and Aaron Elkins. I have written three art world mystery books, *Art is Dead, Going, Going, Gone* and *Art Attack*, each of which focuses on a different aspect of the art world. My protagonist is a Harvard Law School professor. Daniel Silva's is an Israeli secret agent who is a master art restorer. Learning about art isn't a job. It's fun.

There are a lot of art auction houses. At the top are Christie's and Sotheby's. But even they have entry level (for them) auctions and online sales. Phillips is often mentioned in the top group, but not in the same breath.

At the next level are Doyle and Bonham's. Below that is Swann (it leans heavily towards the sale of prints and multiples). All are highly professional. They are mostly divided by the price and the art in which they deal. Of course, there are some overlaps.

Doyle and Bonham's have mixed sales, such as Doyle's Art+Design, which includes collectors' furniture as well as art. Bonham's Made in California sale focuses on California artists. There are some interesting art pieces in these sales and sometimes you can find a bargain. Yesterday I found in the Christie's Design sale (of all places) a marvelous oil and sand work on canvas by Enrico Donati (est. $3000-$5000), a very well collected artist.

Then there are the local auctions. These auctions often concentrate on local artists. In Los Angeles, you have the Los Angeles Modern Auction and the Santa Monica Art Auction, among others.

The major auctions in different categories of art occur at different times of the year. They are seasonal. And many auctions, from the top to the bottom, are grouped around these times. The major auctions in Post-War and Contemporary Art in New York are held in May and November.

Major auctions by the same auction houses in other parts of the world are held at different times throughout the year. These are interesting to look at, but I have never made a purchase through a foreign auction because I don't know the local laws or taxes and I am concerned about the cost of shipping and currency exchange costs.

Then, there are the online auctions that go on during the year at small auction houses throughout the country, some of which have specialized art auctions and some of whom include art among other auction pieces. These are less sought out and may be where you find interesting works. It doesn't cost anything to look.

There are many periods of art from which to choose. We collect Post-War abstract art. We concentrate here because that is what excites us and we have come to know some of the artists and pricing in the area, which is helpful if you are not collecting Cezanne or Jasper Johns.

You can do all your looking online. Every auction and many galleries now put the works of art they have for sale online, even if they issue print catalogs. It is actually a benefit to look at art online. The colors are quite true, in my experience, and the work can often be examined inch by inch with magnification.

The online site will sometimes show the picture in contrast to an individual so you can see the size. The picture will always include the dimension of the piece in inches and often will include the size framed. By the way, most pictures you buy will be framed. Some better than others. So, make sure it fits the wall where you want to hang it.

A 2018 UBS survey reported that of the 175 collectors surveyed, 58% said they bought a work online without ever seeing it in person. That percentage had doubled since 2017.

# Chapter 13

## TIPS ON RESEARCH

So, you want to start research in the area of your interest. Say Western Art. Type it into Google. Look for articles on forgotten or overlooked artists. Keep a list.

Research them on the internet. Read the information on their websites or from galleries dealing in their work. Maybe a catalog from an auction will have an essay about them. Read Wikipedia. Find out who they were.

Look for art magazine articles on or including them. See if there is a *New York Times* obituary. These obituaries are a terrific source of all kinds of information; how the artist was thought of, what museum collections they are in, what place their art has in the art world and who were their contemporaries. You may want to jot down more names.

*The New York Times* is now running an intermittent series of old unpublished obituaries. These sometimes highlight artists, women particularly, who the *Times* feels it has overlooked because it mostly chronicled the death of white men. It just had an obituary of an Indian woman who died in 1941. She was regarded as the Frieda Kahlo of India.

Frieda Kahlo is now considered to be one of Mexico's greatest artists. Her highly imaginative, brooding, and introspective paintings reflect her struggle with a crippling accident and her uneasy marriage to Diego Rivera. Kahlo's work (as well as Rivera's) is fabulously expensive.

Carmen Herrera was never appreciated, although she was a cutting-edge minimalist artist. She was born in Cuba in 1915 and moved to Paris after the end of World War II. Her retrospective at the

Whitney finally led to a recognition that may or may not last. Of course, the price of her art soared. In 2019, Sotheby's sold one of her works for $2.9 million, well above the high estimate.

This suggests another area of possible research. Perhaps a review of retrospectives by significant museums over the last quarter century would be productive. See if the artists have again disappeared from sight. See what prices their work is fetching at recent auctions. It could lead to some interesting opportunities to buy great art on a shoestring.

Hungarian women from the Soviet era are finally coming to international attention. llona Kersu, 84, had her first show in London in 2017. She will be included alongside Carmen Herrera in the Metropolitan Museum's "Epic Abstractions" show.

Alma Thomas had three handicaps. She was Black, she was a woman and she lived in Washington, D.C., not New York. She was an exuberant modernist, whose abstract paintings were filled with disciplined irregular shapes of dense, brilliant colors.

In 2016, the Studio Museum in Harlem and the Tang Teaching Museum at Skidmore mounted her first retrospective in 30 years. In 1972 she had been the first African-American woman to have a full exhibition at the Whitney and promptly was forgotten after her death in 1978.

In 2017, she was included in an exhibition at the National Museum of Women in the Arts along with 20 other women entitled "Magnetic Fields: Expanding American Abstraction, 1960s to Today." The exhibition placed abstract works by multiple generations of Black women artists in context with one another and within the larger history of abstract art.

I never knew there was such a museum. What a wonderful resource.

Or perhaps it would be rewarding to investigate art prizes. A foundation called Art Was a Woman gives cash prizes to under-recognized female artists over 40. It has been doing so for 22 years. That would be a list to check.

Look for past exhibits in your field of interest. Julie Joyce, the curator of Contemporary Art at the Santa Barbara Museum of Art mounted a 2010 show called "Colorscope: Abstract Painting,

1960-1979." It surveyed the progress of Abstract Expressionism from its roots through the first part of its evolution, where color took precedence over expressionistic surface texture. The result was the emergence of Color Field painting, Lyrical Abstract Expressionism and the Hard-Edged painters.

Included in the exhibit were not only Helen Frankenthaler, Hans Hoffman, Bridget Riley and Richard Anuszkiewicz. But also Ernest Posey, Paul Reed, John Seery and Ray Colmer, to name just a few of the artists of whom I had never heard. There were a dozen more. What a rich find.

Paul Reed (1919-2015), who was in that show, was the last surviving member of the Washington Color Field School, which included Morris Louis and Kenneth Noland. A beautiful acrylic on canvas piece came up in the Doyle Fine Modern Art auction in October 2018. I noticed it. The name was familiar. The estimate on the work was $700-$900. We acquired it for $1200 (plus the 25% buyer's commission.) It was a steal.

It can help to get advice. The curators of almost every museum are available to help you. Introduce yourself. Start a relationship.

Curators are the artistic professionals in the museum world. They create the exhibits. They are the scholars.

Curators treasure their field of art. They have dedicated their lives to it. They certainly don't do it for the money. And they love to share.

You do not have to be a big donor. A curator will love your inquisitiveness. They can point you in the right direction because they are in touch with the pulse of the art world. They know a lot. Talk to the curator of your local museum. Tell him or her what you are doing. The curator will help you vet and prune your choices.

Look at pictures of past art exhibitions from museums. Particularly those that focus on artists in which you are interested. Shows of individual artists are good. Exhibits of multiple artists are better since they provide a better survey.

Once you've narrowed your choices, search past art auctions for sales of their works. Are they in your price range for the kind of work you want to acquire? Almost every auction house has an online record of past auctions by name and lot, including the sales price with the buyer's premium included.

There are also numerous online services, such as *Artnet*, which will provide prices and descriptions of the picture sold. These services require a subscription for this information, although basic information is available for free. It may pay to subscribe. You have to decide whether it makes sense for your budget and how much you will spend. They are useful but not critical.

Then start looking at current auctions to see if works in which you're interested are available. Get on mailing lists. Let the auction houses know your interests.

All fellow collectors are not competing with you. They can alert you to pieces they uncover in their own research that are outside their area of interest.

Some artists don't come up at auction often. But in looking you may find other artists you like. Add them to your list. To build a collection of great art on a shoestring, you need to be opportunistic and sometimes need to take a chance. As the satirical pianist, Tom Lehrer, said so well, "Be prepared, that's the Boy Scout's marching song." (He also said some other things in that song that you should probably ignore. But you will laugh out loud.)

Find out which auctions might have works in which you are interested. Auctions are seasonal. Learn the auction dates. Buy a catalogue or finagle one for free. Tell them you are interested. After all, they want to promote interest and bidding. They are happy to help, but remember they have an agenda.

There may be galleries that have, or even specialize in, the kind of art in which you are interested. The Anita Shapolsky Gallery, in an elegant but accessible New York townhouse, is a great source of underappreciated abstract expressionist artists. Shapolsky has an enviable reputation for quality and specializes particularly in women of the '50s and '60s and artists of color.

The gallery recently mounted an exhibit of the work of Ernest Briggs, a second-generation ab-ex artist. Briggs died in 1984. His art expresses a bold, sensual use of form and color, erupting at times into lyrical outbursts. Wow. Never heard of him.

Galleries often ask more than for a similar piece at auction. But galleries have the piece there. Now. You don't have to wait and look. You can negotiate price (yes, most of them will bargain). And you may be able to pay over time without interest.

Occasionally you get a surprise. I discovered Purvis Young in a Doyle auction held on December 1, 2018. Young (1943-2010) was a self-taught black "outsider" artist. We were struck by the power of his art. And he was unknown to me. It shows you what I know.

Young lived his entire life in Overtown, the Black ghetto of Miami. Because he couldn't afford canvas, he painted on every surface available to him. Many of his paintings were on wood scraps. His work was influenced by Van Gogh and Gauguin, whose work he studied in his teens while in prison for armed robbery.

Even as he became more famous, he never thought of leaving Overtown. He said, "I paint what I sees. . .I paint the problems of the world." Over time, he became a cult art figure in Miami, luring art tourists and collectors. He became so important that in 2006 a feature-length documentary on his life was released.

He was included in Metropolitan Museum exhibition of 30 self-taught black artists, "History Refused to Die," that closed in September 2018. Roberta Smith, in *The New York Times*, referred to one of his works as a "masterpiece."

His art is in the permanent collections of the Met, LACMA, the Philadelphia Museum of Art, the Smithsonian and the Corcoran among many others. Wow. He was obviously more recognized than I could imagine.

And his output was massive. Doyle was offering books of works on paper with 30 or 40 paintings for $1500-$2500. We selected an acrylic on board that had an estimate of $900-$1200.

In doing my price research I noted that a lot of galleries on eBay had works for sale at prices that ranged across the board. Some of them seemed great.

For the Doyle auction we put in an absentee bid of $1,600, well above the high estimate. I thought that would be sufficient but we really wanted the piece. We watched the auction live on our computer and I also registered to bid on the internet if I had to.

Anne and I agreed we would go to $2,400, double the high estimate if it were necessary. That committed us to $3,000 (because of the buyer's premium) plus shipping. And we had to bid. We dropped out at $2,400 and the piece went for $2,500.

Darn. But then my research paid off. We looked at the 40 pieces offered on eBay. We found an acrylic on board that was more iconic than the one we bid on and that we liked even more. The gallery in Miami was asking $1,800 including free shipping. I offered $1,500 and they accepted.

This is a rare occurrence. You often cannot find good art on eBay and often the prices are ridiculous. You also face the real question of authenticity. But in this case, Young's art was so cheap and his output was so prodigious, forgery was not an issue. What a great result. All because of research.

Some galleries say they will repurchase, at any time, art you've purchase from them, at your purchase price. If they say so, get it in writing. But even if you get it in writing the gallery must still be in existence and financially solvent when you want to sell. Furthermore, suing to enforce such a guarantee is rarely feasible. These promises are more of a marketing tool than a comfort.

Chapter 14

# The Kinds of Art

For centuries most painting was oil on canvas, or drawings and etchings on paper or parchment. Now there are a large variety of media and surfaces. For our purposes, they are important to understand because they are referenced in the description of art in auction catalogs and galleries.

Oil paint is composed of colors made from minerals ground into a powder (synthetics now) and then mixed with oils. Colors changed as different minerals became available.

Watercolors are pigments suspended in a water solution and applied to paper. The colors are luminescent and most often translucent.

Tempera is the oldest medium, tracing back to ancient Egypt. It is permanent and fast drying, consisting of colored pigments mixed with a glutinous material, such as egg yolk. It was the only paint available until the discovery (or rediscovery) of oil paint in the early fifteenth century. Tempera was used on board and in many wall paintings because it was so long lasting.

Gouache (which is pronounced "gwash") is similar to both watercolors and tempera (not tempura, which is fried Japanese seafood). Gouache is sometimes referred to as opaque water color. It is composed of a high ratio of color pigment, with a binding agent such as gum arabic, and white pigment. It produces a smooth surface, and with layering, vivid colors. It is used almost exclusively on paper.

Acrylic is a permanent, fast drying painting medium made of pigment suspended in an acrylic polymer emulsion. It can resemble oil or watercolor depending on how it is modified. Acrylic paints came into use in the 1950s and have been a common medium of fine art since then. It is popular since it can be modified in more ways than either oil or watercolor, giving an artist more flexibility. It is used on canvas, paper and any other surfaces where oil is used. Painters used it extensively in the 1970s and beyond because it dried more quickly than oil. They liked the colors and since they didn't have to wait as long to apply new layers of paint, it was more efficient.

About everything that will stick to canvas or paper has been used to make art. Dirt, mud and excrement are only a few. Art Brut emphasized the use of such materials.

Canvas and paper are made in various sizes and can be joined together to make diptychs (2 panels) and triptychs (3 panels).

Art has even been made in boxes. Joseph Cornell (1903-1072) is famous for his series of boxes, but he is far from the only one. I own a wonderful box by Marcello Bonevardi (1929-1994), an outstanding Argentine artist.

Color has been applied to a surface in almost every way imaginable. And artists are very imaginative. It was brushed on originally. The palette knife, a flat blade used to apply color thickly in broad flat strokes, was common in the nineteenth century and beyond.

Since the 1940s, paint has been spattered, poked and dripped. It has been applied by turning the canvas or by being mopped or sponged on. Now it is applied using spray cans, fire extinguishers and even through the programing of computers.

A painting can be made on canvas, paper, board, cloth, burlap or any other flat surface. If it is made directly on a wall it is called a mural. If it is made using fresh plaster on a wall or ceiling, it is called a fresco.

Oil paint on canvas or panels is the primary and most valuable art. It can last for hundreds of years. It is durable. Canvas can be raw or smooth, primed with gesso, a thin plaster slip, or not. It still is the art that brings the highest price in painting. Paper disintegrates over time, so it is considered less valuable.

As time went on, paper became better and concerns about

durability lessened. But works on paper are still generally cheaper than works on canvas.

Paper can be hand-laid or commercially produced. It can be rough textured and porous or it can be smooth and non-absorbent. It can be newspaper.

Multimedia art and assemblage are another form of art. Multimedia art may combine painting with glued objects and cut out paper mounted on board or canvas. The cutouts that Henri Matisse executed late in his career are wonderful. The definition of multimedia now includes, among other media, sound, light and digital imagery. Assemblage is what it says. An artist assembles found objects into art.

Collage combines different types of paper, canvas or cutouts into a single piece. Jean Dubuffet made several large paintings that he didn't like. They were put away and ignored. Many years later, Dubuffet decided to cut them apart and combine them into several different pieces of art. Fabulous.

Several artists made torn or cut paper collages. Ronald Bladen (1918-1988), one of the fathers of Minimalism, spent ten years in his studio cutting paper squares, bending the edges up, gluing them on a backing and adding small touches of crayon. I know, but it is a lot better than it sounds. Mark Twain said the same thing about an opera he had just heard. That was a funnier remark.

Ken Noland cut out paper, soaked it, shaped it, painted it and molded it. The piece I saw was beautiful, but someone mounted it on the ugliest backing I have ever seen. Conrad Marco-Relli cut plain burlap into shapes and mounted them on canvas.

We bought all three pieces at auction at attractive prices. We changed the backing on the Noland.

## Chapter 15

## PRINTS AND MULTIPLES

BRONZE SCULPTURE HAS ALWAYS been cast in multiples. Have you ever wondered why so many museums have Rodin's *The Thinker* sitting out in front? Multiples are editions of three-dimensional fine art, as distinguished from prints, which are in two dimensions.

The term "edition" refers to the number of works to be produced in a series. It is determined by the artist, or by the artist and the publisher.

Prints are fine art made in editions, usually on paper, with a variety of different materials deployed in an equally rich range of methods. The reproduction is supervised and the prints are approved by the artist.

Since there are several copies, they are always less expensive than a unique work by the same artist. It may be the only way any of us can own a piece of art by internationally famous artists like Lichtenstein or Frankenthaler.

Originally, prints were hand laid and printed one at a time. They used thick ink. With the advent of offset printing, some prints are made with a much thinner ink and are run off in larger numbers.

Prints may be hand signed or signed in the block. You want hand signed prints. Prints are also numbered in a fraction. The first number is the placement of the print in the series and the second is the size of the series. Aside from the edition of say, 50, there will be artist's proofs and often printer's proofs which will also be separately numbered with a smaller fraction.

There are also monoprints (a single print) with or without hand colored enhancement. There may be several monoprints in different colors.

The four best known print techniques are lithography, etching, screen printing and woodcuts. To create a lithograph, the artist draws on a flat lithographic stone using a grease-based pencil. The stone is then treated so the lines will attract printing ink. A solvent fixes the image.

Ink is applied to the stone and it is placed in a printing press. The image is printed in reverse. Lithography opened up printmaking to artists otherwise reluctant to learn the technical skills needed to create woodcuts or etchings, since many of the same tools, such as brushes and pencils, can be used.

To etch an image, an artist scratches the image onto a metal plate covered in wax, using an etching needle. The plate is then immersed in acid to eat into the exposed metal to fix the image. The plate is inked and cleaned so ink only remains in the etched lines. Then paper is cut to the size of the plate and put on the plate which is put into a press. Etching is a very old technique. People still collect Rembrandt etchings.

In screen printing, a piece of fine mesh is stretched over a frame. The finer the mesh, the sharper the resulting image. The process was originally called silk-screening because silk was used for the mesh. Synthetic material has now replaced silk.

An image is cut into a film or paper, creating a stencil. The stencil is then used to block off parts of the screen. An emulsion is pushed through the screen with a rubber blade. The image appears on the screen which is then used to produce the prints. Andy Warhol is famous for his screen prints.

Woodcut is the oldest printing process. Woodcuts first appeared in ancient China. European woodcut prints with colored blocks were created in the sixteenth century.

The Japanese perfected woodblock printing. Ukiyo-e (ou-ki-yo-e) emerged in the seventeenth century and was a form of art available to the merchant class. It was the people's art of its time. Ukiyo-e means the "floating world," which referred to the world of courtesans and performers.

Most artists had specialized carvers who cut their designs into woodblocks. A separate block had to be carved for each color. There could be as many as 20 colors in a print. The prints are made one at a time by pressing a sheet of paper on the woodblock to create each color in the image.

The great innovation in Ukiyo-e was in locking each block into place to produce clear, multicolor images with sharp lines. Many people, including Vincent Van Gogh and I collected Ukiyo-e. Van Gogh's collection is in the Van Gogh Museum. It is one of the finest collections I have seen.

The value of prints is influenced by the quality of the paper, the integrity of the image and the vibrancy of the colors. Old Master prints are degraded in value if the sheet is trimmed. Of course, the size of the edition (the number of prints made) is important.

There is a myth that a lower edition number is better. 1/50 is better than 47/50. This myth dates back to when copper plates were used to make prints. Copper is a soft metal and the plate would compress and lose detail as it was used again and again. Since the turn of the twentieth century, most, but not all, prints have been made using steel-copper plates that do not deteriorate during the printing process.

Printers are specialists and often artists in their own right. There are some illustrious print houses, including Gemini G.E.L. on the west coast and Long Island Tyler Graphics on the east coast. The quality of the print is a prime determiner of value, so the printer is essential to the process.

The paper that is chosen is also an important part of the artistic expression in print making.

Andy Warhol wanted thinner, cheaper paper for some of his silk screens. It wasn't a decision to save money. It reflected the commercial images he produced and he, perhaps, was thumbing his nose at artistic pretensions.

---

Print collecting is an area of collecting unto itself. It is highly technical and requires a lot of study. It is a worthy pursuit, but not one that appeals to me. We prefer one-of-a-kind works, although I have to admit we have a few multiples in our collection that we acquired early on and still love.

Furthermore, the market for prints is a lot more active and liquid than the market for almost all other art. It is more active because there are editions of prints, so they come up for sale more often. Prices are more transparent. Liquidity means ease of resale and greater demand, which may increase the price. Or not.

# Chapter 16

## BIDDING AND OFFERS

SONIA GECHTOFF WAS A great artist. As I've mentioned, you've never heard of her. Neither had we until we fell in love with one of her paintings and started to do research. Her work is in all the major museums. Not bad for an unknown.

She was represented by major galleries. Her mistake was being born a woman. In 2016, in an article from Artnet N*ews*, she was included in "12 Woman of Abstract Expressionism to Know."

Those 12 women included Lee Krasner, Elaine De Kooning, Helen Frankenthaler and Joan Mitchell, among others (Read the article. It will provide a lot of information and the other women named are not nearly as well known.)

The Gechtoff work I loved was from her later period, hard-edged and subtle. It was not one of her earlier, looser abstracts. Anne loved it too.

We decided to place a bid with the auction house and not participate personally (although we were online for the auction itself in real time and prepared to bid if we were overbid). We had given the auction house a modified Bear Hug bid. A Bear Hug in corporate hostile takeover terms is a bid so high, it scares away any other bidders, so no one will be tempted to join the fray. Our bid was a modified Bear Hug because we didn't open with our maximum bid.

In this case, our maximum bid was well above the high estimate. Remember, the auction house doesn't open the bidding with your maximum bid unless you instruct them to do so. They open the bidding at well below the low estimate and they will sell you the piece when the bidding stops, even if it is below your maximum bid.

An absentee bid is fixed. Since you are not present at the auction, you have no flexibility. If you are placing an absentee bid on a piece with a low estimate, as we were, it makes sense to increase your bid to perhaps double the high estimate with the expectation that the low price will attract bidders (but of course not to more than you are willing to pay to acquire the piece).

If the piece you are interested in appears on the cover of the catalog or is highlighted on the website, expect more competition and revise your bidding strategy accordingly. The placement generates more demand.

Norton Simon was the California industrialist who built Hunt Foods. He became an obsessive art collector, eventually taking over the floundering Pasadena Art Museum and renaming it for himself. He had a strategy for bidding at auction that he employed from time to time.

He would agree with the auctioneer that he was bidding on a designated piece when he got up and left the auction room, until he returned to his seat. Psychologically, he was saying to the other bidders that the work at auction was beneath his notice.

One of the Rothschilds had used a similar ploy on the stock exchange, but with a reverse twist. Rothschild would appear on the floor of the exchange and very obviously begin selling a security. His undisclosed agent would buy up the securities as the price plunged when other traders leapt in, aware of Rothschild's knowledge and reputation.

Coming into the bidding late suggests to other bidders that there is no upper limit to your desire. One knowledgeable collector only enters the bidding when the auctioneers first states "fair warning," after the initial bidders apparently have exhausted their bidding impulses. Another strategy is to instruct your bidder to open the bidding at the high estimate or beyond, "a bear hug bid," if you believe there might be a lot of other bidders and you really want the piece.

Do not try to change the price intervals set by the auction house. They are fixed in most cases. Any bid that does not reflect the interval, say bidding $300 more than the last bid, when the interval is $500, probably will be rejected with scorn. You are changing the momentum of the auction and the auctioneer will not like it.

I tried it once. It was neither pleasant nor successful. The auctioneer paused for a long moment. Then, with distaste, he accepted my bid and announced it was the last bid he would accept from me. The other bidder got the lot at the next increment.

But that was my fault. With all of the good experiences I have had dealing with local auction houses, there is one that was awful. It involved the Hill Auction Gallery in Sunrise, FL. I put in an absentee bid on a piece of art at $900 plus 1. A plus 1 bid assures you that if you are the underbidder at your maximum bid, the auctioneer will place another bid for you at the next bidding increment. It prevents you from being wrong-footed (The last bid by another bidder is equal to your maximum absentee bid. Say your maximum bid is $1,000 but the sequence of bidding allows the opposing bidder to place the bid at $1,000. You would lose the bid by a coincidence. A Plus 1 bid instructs the auctioneer to place another bid at the next increment on your behalf.)

The absentee bid with the plus 1 designation was acknowledged by Hill in writing. Hill did not exercise my plus 1 bid and I lost the lot.

In explanation, I was told by Hill they never accept plus 1 bids. But they had acknowledged it in writing. I left that phone call shaking my head. I was not happy. And there was nothing I could do.

I occasionally buy art from galleries. It is more likely to happen with living contemporary artists. A gallerist (the new term for a dealer) in our small town was well known for refusing to negotiate the asking price of the art he was selling. An unusual practice, but apparently all right for him. But economic circumstances change.

In this case, there was a restaurant attached to the gallery. It was 2009, the height of the economic debacle. Anne and I were having dinner, and before sitting down, we looked through the gallery. There was an oil by Angela Perko, a contemporary artist we both liked.

As we ate, the gallerist came by. We knew him. I asked him flippantly if he would sell me the picture for $4,000, about a 25% discount to his asking price. I expected him to laugh. Instead, he said, "Sure."

The lesson here is to ask. Do it in any way with which you are comfortable. You can always say to a gallerist or artist, "I love this work, but it is out of my price range." See what he or she has to say. You may lose, but you won't be abused. S/he may offer you an extended time to pay or ask your budget. You can't do that at an auction. There is no one to ask.

When you bid at auction, you are stuck with your bid and with the work of art upon which you bid. There is no right to return the piece if you don't like it (this may be different with a gallery) and few rights to complain.

Buying is easy. Resisting the impulse to buy is hard. If you have done the research and have finally concluded on a work you want, you have become emotionally committed to it. You have "seen" it on your wall. The emotion of losing something you "own" is greater than the fear that you overpaid.

If you are disciplined in your bidding, sometimes you will lose. You may lose several times. If you lose a work of art you want, you will suffer a real sense of loss. Someone has taken something that was yours.

It will pass. There are always more great pieces of art. Maybe even better than the one you lost.

Chapter 17

# The Trend

IN THE LAST THREE decades, wealth has flowed to the wealthy. In the United States, the top one-percent of the population own 40% of all the wealth. The top one-tenth of the one-percent alone own more than 20%. Some of them collect art. The number of collectors at the pricier end of the market has been expanding as wealth concentrates.

It only takes two bidders to make an auction. When combined with a competitive urge and the possession of a unique symbol of wealth, the dramatic increase in prices does not come as a surprise.

In 1967, after the death of Alice B. Toklas, the companion of Gertrude Stein, most of Stein's remaining collection came on the market. Gertrude Stein was famous for her Paris salon and all the young artists who she befriended. The remains of her collection included 27 Picassos, seven Juan Gris paintings and a Matisse.

At the urging of Bates Lowry, the director of the Museum of Modern Art at the time, David Rockefeller, with some reluctance, organized a syndicate of five colleagues to bid on the collection. Most were MoMA trustees. When one of them dropped out, Rockefeller took his share.

In September 1968, with the advice of Lowry, the syndicate acquired the entire collection for a total of $6.25 million. It was agreed that six of the major works would ultimately be donated or bequeathed to MoMA.

The collection was shipped to New York, where the art works were cleaned by MoMA's conservators. Then the members of the syndicate gathered in December to distribute by lot the collection among themselves.

For his 2/5 share, about $2.1 million, David Rockefeller acquired, among other works, eight Picasso's including three of the nine most important paintings. Just one, *Young Girl with a Basket of Flowers*, from Picasso's Rose Period (before his Cubist period), sold in May 2018 for $115,000,000. That is an incredible price inflation, even if in 1968 you assign $700,000 (1/3 of the total cost of all the works he was allocated) as the cost of the painting. And he got to live with the painting his entire life.

Many of the works purchased by top-end collectors will never be returned to the market. Most of the best will go to museums. Robert Storr, the professor, curator and critic said, "The function of museums is to make art worthless again."

You need to determine whether art will be an investment, an asset class (where you are hoping to get your money back and perhaps make a profit), or if the value of collecting will be in living with fine art. To some extent, you can have both. But it will change your approach.

Vanessa Selbst, the winningest woman in the history of professional poker, traded in her gaming tables for an office at Bridgewater Associates, a private equity fund in Westport, Connecticut. She was talking here of investment markets, but the same logic applies to the market in art.

"If something's undervalued, does that mean you want to buy? Well, maybe, but if you buy it, how's it going to go up? Who are the other people who are going to buy? What are they thinking about? What's their motivations?" she said, offering an analysis that could fit either an investment, a poker hand or an art auction. "You have to be thinking about who the other players are and what they're going to do." And neither poker nor investments have huge transaction costs or the issues of timing.

There are trends in art, so if you are astute, you might get lucky. It is a lot cheaper and riskier to be ahead of the curve in the art world.

It is a lot riskier and a lot more expensive to be behind the curve. To collect in the market, you need to determine where and when you will play and how to improve your chances. That is, if your purchase of art is to be an investment.

In the art market, it is said that to find out what is going on, look at the auction day sales, not the evening extravaganzas. Loic Gouzer, formerly of Christie's, observed at the end of 2018 that the art market is not in a bubble. It is strong, with huge prices in the evening sales, because the major auction houses tend to focus on the artists that are doing well at a specific time. It is a selective sample. They don't talk about those who are lagging.

In the day sales, the market has been stagnating for the last 10 years, according to Artnet *News*. Only contemporary works have increased in value (they define contemporary as work by artists born in 1945 or thereafter). Low estimates on their work has increased nearly 70% in the last decade, from $92,000 a lot in 2008, to $156,000 a lot in November 2018. Post-war, impressionist and modern art have not regained their 2008 peaks.

And the increase in contemporary art prices has filtered into the lower end of the market as well. The price of emerging artists has also risen.

In 2014, the art dealer and collector Niels Kantor paid $100,000 for an abstract oil on canvas by Hugh Scott-Douglas, a 27-year-old emerging artist. He had on his dealer's hat. He expected to flip it at a profit.

Oops. He sold it in 2016, through Phillips, for $20,000. "I feel like it…(could) go to zero," he said. The prices for Scott-Douglas and Lucien Smith, another young artist, had soared since 2014. Then they crashed.

Smith made a painting in his early 20s, while still a student, that sold at Philips in 2013 for $389,000. Two years earlier it was purchased for $10,000. In 2016, the estimates for his work were as low as $7,000.

2016 was the year of a big readjustment. "Everyone got stuck with their pants down," Kantor said (in his underwear).

If you are a collector, you will improve your chance of acquiring good art works that will retain their attraction over time, whether or not they increase in value. The challenges of the investor are just different. You need to acquire art for which there is an active resale market and that can absorb the high cost of sale.

Trends require research. In a *New York Times* article, a major British art consultant was quoted as saying that the last decade was all about finding hot young artists. But now, the consultant said, it has changed. It's about finding forgotten artists.

The market for Outsider Art is heating up at the moment. The Metropolitan Museum recently mounted a major exhibition of Black Outsider Art selected from pieces donated to it by the Souls Grown Deep Foundation. (The Foundation is dedicated to documenting and preserving the contributions of artists from the African-American South. The artists in is collection are worth looking at.) No one knows how long this trend will continue. But for now, it seems quite strong.

Read your art magazines. Speak to professionals. Ask questions. Pay attention. It is all part of the passion, and it is fun.

If recouping your purchase price (and who can fault you for that) is important to your decision to collect, consider collecting prints by internationally known artists. The branding creates demand and demand creates liquidity. The market is bigger.

Or now, you can even buy a small share of a major work of art. I was offered a share in a Monet recently. And NASDAQ just announced that a Chinese company is offering listed shares in Michelangelo's *Crucifixion*. Shares listed on a stock exchange can be bought and sold on a daily basis with minimal cost.

We own a huge Lichtenstein print from his Perfect/Imperfect series. We bought it early and still love it. The Lichtenstein print is clearly more salable than some great paintings we own by artists who have been forgotten. We could probably sell it at a profit.

And there are some great prints. But interestingly, collecting great prints would not fit with our sense of adventure. Or our economics. Prints by internationally famous artists tend to be more expensive than the unique pieces we seek.

# Chapter 18

## THE PRICING OF CONTEMPORARY ART

THE MERELY RICH HAVE been priced out of the top end of the Modern and Post-War art markets. Certainly, out of the Impressionist market. That, in turn, has led to a thriving market for hot contemporary art. There, they can be big fish in a smaller, splashy pond.

The auction houses, very conscious of the trend, have fed it to their success. The Contemporary Art market has been called a run-away train. Art experts and critics search for the next great young artist. Some artists now can actually make a good living. Damien Hirst and Jeff Koons certainly have.

The question of the long-term value of any contemporary art or artist will only be determined as history looks back over the great, sparkling river of art that flows through the jungle of the art world. Is the artist a boulder diverting the flow, a small rock making a ripple, or a pebble, down somewhere deep beneath the surface?

The auction estimates of the value of a piece of art, and its ultimate purchase price, is determined by many factors, both rational and subjective. Stefan Edles, an important collector, paraphrasing Oscar Wilde, said "There's a lot of people who know the price of everything and the value of nothing."

How much of the estimate (or the asking price) is publicity driven, personality based or whimsy? Surely, no one knows. Peter Schjeldahl, in an essay in *The New Yorker*, said "Auction antics hardly amount to historical verdicts, but, these days, trying to ignore the market when discussing artistic values is like trying to communicate by whisper at a Trump rally."

In contemporary art, the emergence of the artist as a celebrity further clouds the issue of the living artist's place in the artistic firmament. And it is sometimes difficult to distinguish between being on the cutting edge and being bamboozled. How does the market cope with a young artist who can create fifty variations of a computer-based art work in an hour?

Obviously, the perceived quality of the work is important. A strong piece should sell for a great deal more than a weak one. Works from a specific series of an artist's *oeuvre* (his or her complete body of work) may bring more than another, because the former may seem more seminal to the artist's development.

Provenance can make a difference. Ownership by a celebrity or a noted museum can increase the value dramatically. So can regard for the artist at the time by critics or a previous sale by a brand-name gallery. Branded galleries are the first-tier galleries, who handle the most famous artists. They can raise an artist's price simply by representing him (or her). Gagosian is a branded gallery, as are White Cube, Hauser & Wirth and Pace.

It is said the Impressionists are so popular because they are accessible. Anne and I gravitate to what one of our friends describes as "happy art." And all that is before you reach the question of artistic merit.

Well, dang it, maybe you should just buy what you like. But without the research to support your emotional response, how can you know the quality of the work? How can you be sure what you like is good? Or important. Or priced right? Do you have the knowledge?

Branding provides an alternative. Branding is a short-cut. What the rich want to acquire is what economists refer to as positional goods that prove they are rich and knowledgeable. That requires a brand name and a recognizable style.

As Loic Gouzer, formerly of Christie's, observed in an interview with *artnet News'* Andrew Goldstein in December of 2018, "there is a great deal of uncertainty about the art market." And while he does not believe the art market is in a bubble, what he sees as "not very healthy, is the fact that the power of brands is becoming overwhelming."

Art is a luxury item. With all luxury items, branding is critical. It is the brand that connotes wealth or sophistication to people who may not know quality.

You can deal with a branded gallery. Galleries are often, but not always, more expensive than an auction for a similar piece. You may be able to pay over time without interest. You may even be able to bargain. An auction, if you win, is cash before delivery.

Branded contemporary artists are another choice. They are the artists everyone is talking about. They sell at rising prices in auctions or galleries and are well thought of by the art press.

Cicely Brown was born in London in 1969. In 1995, the year Brown relocated to New York, the art world took notice of her when she displayed *Four Letter Heaven* at the Telluride Film Festival, which was shown in the United States as well as Europe. Sexuality and pornography are themes she explores in the film as well as the rest of her body of work.

The sexuality and eroticism of Brown's depictions of expressive figures and nudes are echoed in rich colors, vibrant paint handling, and animated brushwork. She has received a lot of critical attention for powerful, large canvases and bold brushwork. Gagosian has represented Brown for 20 years.

Demand for Brown's paintings shot up in 2018. Five or her 10 top auction results were achieved in that year, including a record $6.8 million sale at Sotheby's. With a total of $19.7 million in sales in the first half of 2018, Brown came in 10th on the list of best-selling artists.

All art sells on the basis of supply and demand, just as do other material goods. Branding affects demand. If the reputation of the artist or the gallery or the auction house can increase demand, the price will rise. The supply is restricted because an art work is unique and imposes a partial limit on supply (not a complete limit since there are other works by the same artist of similar quality that are probably available for sale).

Recently, the journal *Science* published a three-year study that argues that a living artist's financial and critical success primarily results from early approval from the art world's most exclusive gatekeepers. The study mapped half a million international artists through hundreds of thousands of galleries, museums and auctions for 26 years.

They ranked each venue (expressed in the form of balloons) by its prestige level. For example, MoMA's is much bigger than the Whitney, which in turn is bigger than the Contemporain de Montreal. The Pace Gallery receives a larger balloon than the Paul Kasmin Gallery. They mapped out a network demonstrating which galleries and museums tended to show the same artists.

From there, the researchers analyzed how artists careers progressed, based on where in the ecosystem they managed to gain traction at an early stage of their careers. The study determined that 39% of the artists whose first five exhibition put them in the upper echelon of the system were still actively exhibiting 10 years later, mostly in high prestige venues. And practically none ended their careers on the fringe.

In contrast, only 14% of artists who started in lower prestige venues were exhibiting a decade later. And only a little over 1% managed to infiltrate the celestial venues by the end of their career.

Of course, the study was an economic and critical survey, not one of quality. But it does tell us that if you are collecting contemporary art by living artists, the smart play is to start at the top and pay the premium for the brand in order to increase your chance of a return on your investment.

It is all this uncertainty that drove me to approach the market on a more analytical basis. I was insecure. And it is how I discovered, over time, how many great artists have been forgotten and their art ignored since they have died.

## Chapter 19

## WHAT YOU NEED TO KNOW

SELLING ART IS A BUSINESS. Buying art is a passion. The catalog for an auction is an agreement. As with all business agreements, read the fine print. It is illuminating. Some of the most interesting things show up in the footnotes.

When a catalog names Picasso as the artist who created the painting, the auction house believes he painted the work. There is no modifier before the name. Read on.

If a painting is "attributed to" Picasso, the auction house is giving its qualified opinion that the work is by Picasso, but for some reason, it is not certain. If they aren't certain, how can you be? Don't buy it.

If the catalog says "after," that is an art work done in the style of another artist. "School of" means it was painted by the artist's team, usually referring to art of the Renaissance through the early nineteenth century. They don't do that with Damian Hirst or Andy Warhol.

For our collection, Anne and I only purchase art with unqualified attribution. We once put in a written bid for a work by Carman Herrera. When I went back to look at the catalog, I noticed that the auction house had added "attributed to." We withdrew our bid since the auction had not yet taken place.

You will see a reference to a catalogue raisonne' in the description of some lots. A catalogue raisonne' is a comprehensive listing, with notations and images, if possible, of all the known work by an artist. The intention is to allow a third party to identify a work as part of the artists *oeuvre*. To authenticate it.

It requires an immense amount of work, years of effort, to compile, so only the most important artists are afforded such publication. It took 11 years to compile the catalogue raisonne' of Robert Motherwell.

Galleries used to be responsible for the creation of a catalogue raisonne' for their important artists. Now it is often a charitable foundation created by or for an artist that sponsors the creation. *The New York Times* has described catalogues raisonne' as the definitive, scholarly, compendia of an artist's work, the supreme arbiter of genuine versus fake. Inclusion in such a catalogue has a critical impact on the value of a work.

And a catalogue raisonne' is a living document in the sense that lost work may be discovered and authenticated. A great deal of effort is made to have a discovered work authenticated and included in the catalogue raisonne' for obvious reasons. However, many foundations will no longer opine on the authenticity of a purported work because of the potential litigation and liability that may ensue. Some foundations may even refuse to publish new editions of a catalogue raisonne'.

But, fear not. In a capitalistic world a vacuum cannot long exist if someone can figure out a way to make money. Art dealer Richard Polsky is now offering an authentication service for the works of Jackson Pollack (along with those of Jean-Michel Basquiat, Andy Warhol and Keith Haring). Pollack fakes continue to crop up. Pollack is, perhaps, the most forged Post-War artist.

Polsky offers collectors a two-step approach. For $2,500 he will examine and research the work to determine, in his opinion, if the work may be genuine. If there is a high probability of authenticity, his service will then, at the request of the owner, refer the work to an independent laboratory for scientific examination.

While this process is not the equivalent of authentication by the artist's foundation, it may go a considerable distance towards creating market acceptance. That means the sale price will be higher.

The International Foundation of Art Research has published a database of catalogues raisonne'. A separate database exists for catalogues in preparation. These catalogues can be searched electronically. Another database on a separate site, in searchable form, exists for catalogues raisonne' of prints.

Occasionally, an auction house will offer art it owns in an auction. There is an inherent conflict of interest that can affect the estimated value ascribed to the piece, no matter how pure the house's motives. Such a lot will be identified by a symbol in the catalog, as will a lot upon which the house has given a guarantee, which creates the same issue.

A guarantee assures the seller of a minimum price and sometimes the auction house may have to give one to receive the consignment of the work. Since this only happens with major works or major collections that are considered imperative to its auction, it is not something Anne and I need worry about in our collecting.

There is an interesting variation on a guarantee at art fairs and they don't have to tell you. A dealer may have a painting "pre-sold" before the fair. If he sells it for more during the fair, he splits the upside with the "guarantor." This permits the dealer to bring more inventory to the fair without risk. It also limits his need to negotiate, which enhances his stature.

If anyone in an auction has a reason for bidding up the price, such as a third-party guarantor, that should be disclosed. There should be a symbol by the lot. Look for it.

Any statement by an auction house is in their honest opinion. The bigger auction houses do in-depth research on important lots. That includes, importantly, their report on condition and the authenticity of the art work. But they don't guarantee it. Warranties are strictly limited. And the auction house can be wrong.

Between 2009 and 2011 the hedge-fund manager and collector Andrew Hall bought 24 works by Leon Golub. He purchased six of them through Christie's, Sotheby's and Artnet auctions (the others he bought from the owners of the paintings directly, (thereby avoiding the buyer's premium).

In 2015, he asked the Golub Foundation to examine the works and the foundation immediately responded that there was no record of the works being those of Golub. These were sophisticated fakes, fooling everyone, but on closer examination, there were clear issues in style and form. There was none of the painstaking scraping of paint that marked Golub's style.

And estimates of value are just that. You need to do your own research. We wanted to bid on a piece by Ronald Bladen at a Christie's auction. Bladen was a father of Minimalism. The particular piece consisted of folded squares of brown paper with black crayon.

My price research did not support the much higher estimate. Perhaps it was because works by Bladen don't appear at auction often. Our bidding was very much influenced by my research. We acquired the piece, as I expected, below the low estimate.

Lots are sold "as is." Essentially, you're stuck. But an auction house may move to rescind a sale if questions of authenticity arise thereafter. That means the auction house can take back the piece and return your money, whether or not the you demand it.

There is an authenticity warranty to protect the buyer. But, it is very narrow, and the only remedy is rescission. The buyer may initiate such a claim, but only within a limited contractual period. And the buyer must prove that the work is not authentic. If questions of authenticity don't arise for years, it may be too late.

If there is a rescission, two things then occur. The buyer gets his purchase price back. Not any appreciation in value, if that has occurred. Not sales tax or shipping. Nor any costs of making the claim. And, second, the value of the art is irretrievably damaged.

In a case of a rescission, Sotheby's determined an Old Master painting it sold was a fake and issued a refund. The seller was on the hook. Lionel de Saint Donat-Pourrieres was held in breach of the contract of his consignment to Sotheby's and ordered to repay $1.2 million, including interest and attorney's fees.

The purported Parmigianino, sold in 2012, came under suspicion in 2016, when the French authorities mounted a raid on an exhibition and seized several works that were suspected forgeries. The suspected paintings came to market, as did the painting sold by the auction house, through Giuliano Ruffini.

Ruffini was a French collector at the center of a major Old Masters scandal. Paintings sold by him had fooled auction houses and world-class museums. A technical analysis of the picture Sotheby's sold revealed materials unavailable at the time the artist lived. Sotheby's protected its reputation and the seller, literally, paid the price. If, of course, Sotheby's can collect.

In 2011, Sotheby's had also sold a supposed Frans Hals from Ruffini for $10 million in a private sale. It has refunded the purchase price and is suing the gallery that bought the painting from Ruffini.

As Artnet *News* said "it is undoubtedly troubling that so many fake paintings could pass muster at the leading auction houses…."

---

In addition to the hammer price and the buyer's premium, you will be required to pay sales tax on both. Sales tax can be an expensive addition to cost and you have to keep that in mind. It is one of the unrecoverable additions to price you will incur. When you go to sell the piece, no one will count the sales tax in determining value.

You do not have to pay sales tax in the state of the auction if you have the art delivered to another state. If that state has no sales tax, none is due.

As art sales are climbing world-wide and collectors run out of space, the question of where to store art has become more pressing. Storage companies are scrambling to keep up with the demand and facilities are expanding, while new ones are opening. There are now millions of square feet of art storage around the world.

In your exploration of the art world, you will soon run across the term "freeport." Freeports came into existence because of taxes. These are large storage complexes built in free trade zones created by a political entity. The purchase of art can result in a large amount of sales tax. There are also custom and import duties if art is shipped from one country to another.

Delaware, which has no sales tax, has begun branding itself as an art freeport in the United States. But the largest, most secure, and certainly the most secret is in Geneva, Switzerland.

Art sent to a tax-free destination does not trigger any tax or duties until it reaches its final destination beyond the freeport, even if the art is stored there on a long-term basis. Many works of art are stored in crates, so the operators of the storage facility have no idea of what is inside. It has been speculated that a good deal of stolen art is in the Geneva freeport.

Certainly, many art works have been bought and sold without ever leaving the freeport. They are just carried to a new space and no tax is due, to be held there for the next sale.

But be careful. Dennis Kowzlowski, the notorious former chief executive of Tyco International (who went to jail for stealing $600 million from his company), tried to avoid New York sales tax on the $13 million he paid for a Renoir and a Monet to hang in his 13-room New York apartment. He had the paintings delivered to the corporate headquarters of Tyco in Exeter, New Hampshire. New Hampshire doesn't have a sales tax.

Then he had them shipped back to him in New York. His indictment in 2002 was the first charge in an ongoing investigation that cascaded into his ultimate downfall. And he paid New York $3.2 million in back sales tax, interest and penalties.

Just as you must be aware of sales tax, you also need to be aware of local laws that can impact the price of your art. A federal appeals court recently ruled that visual artists are no longer entitled to royalties from the resale of their art in California under a 1977 law, the "California Resale Royalties Act." Artists had earned 5% of the price of any resale. I was totally flummoxed to discover there was ever such a law.

The California law addressed an important issue in the art world. It allowed an artist to participate in the increasing value of his or her art, a problem that has frustrated artists for years.

Robert and Ethel Scull were taxi tycoons. They started buying droves of Ab-Ex and Pop art in the 1960s and 1970s. They wanted to have the position that important collectors claim in the Manhattan social scene. A position mere money can't buy. Tom Wolfe called them "the folk heroes of every social climber who ever hit New York." But they seem to have been possessed of either excellent taste or extraordinary luck, or maybe both.

The Sculls resold 50 of their best paintings for a huge profit at Sotheby's in 1973. The sale has become famous as a turning point in the price of contemporary art.

Robert Rauschenberg, who had sold them his painting *Thaw* for $900, was incensed when he saw it sell for $85,000 and witnessed Robert Scull celebrating. He confronted Scull, shoving him, some say hitting him, and claiming that Scull was exploiting artists.

The California Resale Royalties Act stemmed from the French concept of *droit de suite* and variations have been enacted all over the world. I never imagined that California had one. Now, no state in the United States has such a law.

You also need to get the art from the auction house to your home. Professional packing and shipping are required. Shipping is not usually too expensive but can increase if the work is large or needs to be crated. I have paid over a $1,000 for shipping and as little as $150. You need to know the cost and include it into your calculation of the total cost of the art.

All of the auction houses have a recommended list of shippers with whom they have worked and who are experienced in shipping art. Get two bids. While the estimates may be close, you never know.

Chapter 20

## THE GREAT AUCTION HOUSES

ON A GOOD EVENING in New York, with lots of great art and wealthy collectors, an Impressionist and Modern Art evening auction at Sotheby's or Christie's is the blood sport of high society. It is there that commerce and avarice bend the knee of fealty to art. (To bend the knee of fealty to your lord, in old English, is to "attorn." That is where the term "attorney" comes from. Perhaps that says something.)

Auction houses are really analysts and brokers in a specialized field of marketing. The auction house has advertised the sale. They have contacted potential collectors from all over the world (there are probably only about 500 collectors out of six billion people who play in the major leagues) and have toured the best pieces to all their worldwide showrooms so collectors can view the works.

They will have produced a beautiful color catalog which they have sent to important (and not so important) buyers. There will not only be pictures of the treasures that they are offering, but there will be scholarly entries on some of the more noted pieces.

The auction room is large, with comfortable but not plush, movable chairs. The walls are paneled, as bespeaks a night when hundreds of millions of dollars will change hands. If the auction house has made large guarantees on certain pieces, the executives of the house might be fretting and uneasy. Tums will be popped.

The auctioneer is the ring-master of this particular circus. He (most of the auctioneers at the highest end are men) is a consummate showman, debonair and charming. The Brits seem to have a lock on the high end of the business. Think of a cross between Laurence Olivier and P.T. Barnum.

The auctioneer is never introduced by name, but everyone knows him. This anonymity, combined with subtle familiarity, is important to the impression that he is just a facilitator of the bidding, not someone who seeks to influence it, which he does. God forbid he should be seen as a salesman.

The best auctioneer is a performer. He seeks to establish a rhythm and a mood to encourage participation and raise enthusiasm. He can use humor and stress to seek remarkable bids from the audience.

He wields his gavel like a symphony conductor's baton. There is no time that lasts so long as the time between when an auctioneer says he will sell unless there is a higher bid, "fair warning," and when he strikes his gavel on the podium and says "sold." It is a true measure of the malleability of time.

At its most elevated level, an auction is the ultimate upper-end sport. At many auctions, there are only two dozen people out of hundreds, who actually come to bid.

The auctioneer must control the room as a conductor controls an orchestra. Auctions are exciting. Your adrenaline surges. Your heart beats faster. You become completely focused if you are bidding. It is thrilling, even just to be there. You hold your breath.

The gavel's rap ending the bidding is a small punishment to those who have disappointed him. The auctioneer will often acknowledge the winning bidder, in rare cases by name, more often by location or dress, in a congratulatory nod to the bidder's wisdom. When an art work sells for a hundred million dollars the room breaks into applause.

At some of the high-end auctions, you can't get a ticket. The auction house has carefully selected the audience. The evening must be just so, with a mix of elegant society and the filthy rich.

For one such sale at Sotheby's, the mandated dress was tuxedo, an audacious demand. The auction was preceded by a lavish party with champagne, caviar and foie gras. It was rare, but the auction house was pulling out all the stops. It had a guarantee of hundreds of millions of dollars on the collection that was to be sold.

Who wouldn't want a guarantee if you could get one? A guarantee is not readily available in any market. After all, a guarantee entails a substantial risk. One real estate guy I know told me a guarantor was a schmuck with a pen. True, the context was a little different. Think of a guarantee as really a fixed bid to buy an art work at auction.

A guarantee accomplishes three important objectives. First, it assures the seller that the art will be sold at the amount of the guarantee or more. Second, and perhaps even more important, it avoids the work being "bought in" (not selling). A bought in piece is either sold privately at a distressed price, or it is held for several more years. It is "shopworn" and shopworn art is not auctioned again until the market forgets.

Finally, a guarantee burnishes the desirability of the painting. Someone thought a lot of the quality of the art to risk guaranteeing its sale. A major work does not come to auction without a guarantee. As Artnet *News* said, "Like getting a useful cold call from a telemarketer, it just doesn't happen."

Well, as it turns out, that is not always true. In an example that stunned the art world, the billionaire currency trader, Joe Lewis, turned down a guarantee on David Hockney's "Portrait of an Artist (Pool with Two Figures) (1972), an enigmatic painting of a man swimming, being watched by a man in a pink jacket, that he consigned to Christie's for its 2018 fall sale.

It's not that he couldn't get one. Apparently, guarantees in the range of $70 million were available. He also refused to set a reserve price. That meant the work would be sold to the highest bidder, no matter what the final bid, even if it were far below the estimated value. Apparently, the Hockney went to the auction block naked. It was unheard of.

But a guarantee comes at a cost. If the picture is bid in below the guaranteed price, the guarantor receives a fixed fee (and the painting) in return for his payment of the guaranteed amount. In other words, he bought the painting for the guaranteed price less his fee. If it is sold above the guaranteed price, the guarantor participates in the excess.

Christie's was seeking $80 million or more for the Hockney. In context, the auction record for a Hockney painting was $28.4 million set in 1990 at a Sotheby's auction. The most expensive work for a living artist was set in 2013 when a buyer paid $58.4 million for a piece by Jeff Koons.

Any currency trader is a gambler and one who can assess risk. And he can do it successfully if he is worth a billion dollars. If you believe in the value of your art, why dilute the profit?

And, if you are really wealthy, maybe this is a bet that would not be life altering if you lost. Since there was no reserve, the painting would be sold, maybe for $50 million or $60 million. Lewis would lose $10 million or $20 million. So what.

And everyone was talking about the painting because of the shocking way it came to the block. It stimulated demand. Someone could hope for a bargain.

On November 15th, 2018, at Christie's Post-War and Contemporary Evening Sale, nine bidders pursued the Hockney. Finally, it came down to two bidders on the telephone. After nine minutes of spirited bidding, *Portrait of an Artist (Pool with Two Figures)* sold for $90.3 million dollars to enthusiastic applause and Joe Lewis won his bet, going away. The buyer was unidentified.

As is typically the case, in this auction the first lots were carefully ordered and given deliberately low estimates to induce bidding and create a sense of excitement. It was like throwing chum in the water for the sharks. The auctioneer was also trying to set the tempo of bidding.

Sotheby's was founded in London in the mid-eighteenth century. Sotheby's great rival, Christie's, was founded 20 years later.

Sotheby's may not have created, but most certainly contributed to, the rise of art as an asset class. The creation of the idea of art as an investment that could be pursued for profit.

In 1966, Peter Wilson, the then chairman of Sotheby's confidently declared, "Works of art have proved to be the best investment, better than the majority of stocks and shares in the last 30 years." Wilson was committed to bringing newly wealthy buyers into the market.

He was a business man. He wanted to increase demand. The higher the sales price, the greater the commission.

In a marketing coup, in 1967 he convinced the *Times* of London to publish the Times-Sotheby's Index, an index that purported to chart the price of art sold at auction. The graphs that appeared gave the prices the trustworthy appearance of the stock prices on the financial pages.

Robert Hughes in his 1984 essay observed, "Our culture has been schooled to think of works of art as investment commodities. I think of it as beginning with a curious enterprise called the Times-Sotheby's Art Indexes."

Sotheby's and Christie's share the first rank among fine art auctioneers and are responsible for the vast majority of art sales by dollar. And that led to scandal.

In 1982, the real estate mogul and financier Alfred Taubman took over Sotheby's and became its Chairman. In the mid-1980s, in a series of highly secret meetings, a deal was struck between Diana Brooks, the CEO of Sotheby's and Christopher Davidge, the CEO of Christie's, to fix commission rates. That is a big no-no.

When an antitrust investigation was initiated, Mr. Davidge secured amnesty when he fessed up and delivered extensive documentation to the authorities, implicating Sotheby's. Ms. Brooks rolled over on Mr. Taubman.

Christie's and Sotheby's paid a settlement of over $500 million to their clients. Sir Anthony Tennant, the chairman of Christie's, fled to England.

Mr. Taubman, who seems to have been the odd man out in this game of musical chairs, went to jail. Not the happiest ending for an enormously successful billionaire, owning, at least in his world, a prize better than the Dallas Cowboys.

As my former boss, Mickey Rudin, Frank Sinatra's lawyer, once wrote to a client (not Frank) who had proposed a questionable scheme, "I can get you a telephone, but you won't like the food."

# Chapter 21

## THE ART WORLD

THE ART WORLD IS a loose network of overlapping subcultures held together by a belief in art. It consists of artists, dealers, galleries, collectors, museums, art fairs, auction houses, art professionals, critics, writers, advisors and many others. The art world is individuals. There is no "center" to the art world any more. It exists across time as well as space. It exists physically, intellectually and on the internet. It is what you want it to be.

I was shocked to learn that artists are not important in the art world. I better clarify that quickly. Of course, there would be no art without artists. Collectively, they are essential.

Individually, they are not. Art flows over time. And the flow, like a river, is always changing. The old Chinese proverb is that a man can never cross the same river twice, for when he returns, he is different and the river is different.

Living artists pour their art into the stream. Some will be poster boys (or girls), lifted onto the shoulders of collectors, critics and museums for a time. Hailed and celebrated like a victorious Roman general. The vast majority won't. Even for those that are raised up, many fall, or more likely, will be shoved off.

But time is the judge. The great artists shape and divert the flow. But, the art world is the whole of it, not the artist.

Art is subject to fads. It is an emotional business, as well as an economic one. Old Masters have fallen out of favor. Contemporary art is in. Warhol is great. Paul Jenkins is not. All of this emotion and the harsh hand of history, together with the rise and fall of the world economy, govern the commercial heart of the market.

Along with the museums. They have the audacity to buy up (at least a few of the rich ones do), or beg (most), all the good stuff, the masterpieces. And they have a lot of time to do it in, slowly and sometimes, not so slowly. Once the art is swallowed up, it will never return to the market. At least very rarely, and never the best.

---

Museums haven't always been around. These "egalitarian" institutions didn't arise until the middle of the eighteenth century as royalty fell and their art became public property.

Before that, art was in churches or in the palaces of the nobility. Artists had to have patrons. Those patrons were the nobility or the Church. The Medici were renowned patrons.

That was where the money was and artists had to make a living. He who has the gold makes the rules. So, what was painted was what pleased the patron. And the art was seen only by the patron and his guests.

Some art owned by the Church could be seen in the grander churches and cathedrals if you were of sufficient stature to attend. But art was instructive or for the greater glory of God. You must listen to the priest, not just stare at the art.

The modern museum movement in the United States arose from the wealth of the robber barons of the Golden Age at the end of the nineteenth century. As these men grew immensely wealthy, many longed for social standing among their peers and among European sophisticates who regarded most Americans as rubes.

The players have changed, but the game remains essentially the same, even today. There is little as stirring as sitting in someone's dining room, under a real museum-quality painting.

In the Golden Age, fine art, particularly Old Masters, provided an avenue (coaxed along by a few dealers in New York, like Duveen, who wanted to make money) for these oligarchs. Collecting art became a show of prestige, wealth and sophistication.

Mellon, Morgan and many others toured Europe, with their dealers and advisors in tow, to buy art. They bought it in droves. They vacuumed up the available art, some great, some not so great, much to the annoyance of the Europeans. An increase in demand for a limited market of goods increased the price. It still does.

Perhaps because of income taxes, or perhaps because of a desire for immortality (that wasn't based on an accident of birth or on the teachings of the immortal Church), these rich men founded museums. Some named the museums for themselves (The Frick). Some, like Mellon, took a different view. Mellon founded the National Gallery of Art in Washington.

There are other national museums in Washington, like the Smithsonian and the Hirschhorn, that bear the names of their founders. But Mellon wanted other wealthy men to contribute without feeling they were contributing to his glory, rather than that of the nation. It was a rare act of selflessness among a group of men scarcely known for their lack of ego.

Most paintings are not purchased by museums. Far and away, the source of great art available to us today is the contributions to museums from collectors. And museums in the last 50 years have gravitated from their scholarly and elitist roles to become more accessible and people friendly. They wanted to reach out, but they also needed the money.

Collectors are a critical part of art. They finance the creation of art and support the museums. But where does that leave the poor (rich) collector? Nothing good is left, so they better find an area of art that hasn't been picked over.

When something "good" comes on the market, it creates a frenzy. The *Salvator Mundi*, Leonardo's painting that sold at Christie's in 2017 for $450,000,000, was not in pristine condition. It was damaged and overpainted. It had been heavily restored (which was not unusual for an Old Master). But according to a scholar who examined the work, there was enough there to convey an excellent impression. It must have been really excellent. Christie's pre-sale estimate was $100,000,000.

The painting has an interesting history. As reported in *The Wall*

*Street Journal*, the *Salvator Mundi* hung in the Baton Rouge home of Basil Clovis Hendry, Sr. for years. He inherited the work from his aunt, Minnie Stanfill Kuntz in 1987. He had no idea of the importance of the painting. In 2004, the children of Hendry inherited the estate, including the Leonardo.

Apparently, the Kuntzs bought the painting through Sotheby's in 1958 from the estate of Sir Francis Cook. They paid 45 British Pounds, the equivalent of about $120.

Two dealers, Robert Simon and Alexander Parrish, bought the work from the estate of Basil Hendry in 2005 for less than $10,000 (the auction estimate was $1200-$1800). The dealers obviously saw something in the work that interested them.

They teamed up with a few other dealers to have the painting cleaned and studied by a leading scholar. After the scholar realized the work might be a Da Vinci, the dealers took it to a host of curators to seek validation, which they eventually received.

But the story doesn't stop there. In 2013, the Swiss art advisor, Yves Bouvier, bought the painting from the dealers for $80,000,000. He then immediately resold it to his client the Russian billionaire Dmitry Rybolovlev for $127,000,000.

When Mr. Rybolovlev learned of the mark up, he sued Mr. Bouvier, contending Mr. Bouvier was his agent working on commission, not a dealer. The litigation has continued for years and has not been concluded.

Mr. Rybolovlev maneuvered to have the Principality of Monaco file criminal fraud charges against Mr. Bouvier. Mr. Bouvier, in his turn, caused Monaco to investigate that decision. Mr. Rybolovlev was arrested in Monaco for bribery. He is now free on bail.

Mr. Rybolovlev offloaded the work at Christie's last year for the $450,000,000 price (a bit above the $100,000,000 estimate). While that doesn't really affect Mr. Rybolovlev's claim against Mr. Bouvier (which is based on contract), it certainly makes it a lot less sympathetic.

In any case, most of us are not in the awkward position of having even a $100,000,000. That isn't enough to buy a sports team. Not even close. You can make a donation, but not enough to have a school named after you (maybe a building or a plaza). Perhaps you can buy a share in a jet plane. A house or two in nice places. But a lot of other people can do that, too.

You can play in the art market. Well, there's no way you're going to get a good Van Gogh. Not even a bad one (and there are some.) Picasso is out. A fine Leger oil will set you back $30,000,000. Too much. And they've all been picked over by the museums.

Pollack and Rothko are as expensive as Picasso. And there are all those forgeries. Perhaps a nice big Morris Louis for $1,000,000. That's closer. But will your friends know who Morris Louis is? It is a tough life to have so little money.

But what if you don't have $1,000,000 for a painting, or Heaven forbid, even for a whole collection. You can still collect great art.

## Chapter 22

## A Brief Romp Through Recent Art History

LET ME PRESENT A short and incomplete survey of the art movements of recent years. These art movements overlap in time and artists are often identified with more than one movement. But the history of art is an important source of knowledge in collecting. It is far more complex than I can hope to convey in a short chapter.

Movements seem to occur as a new generation of artists become restless and revolt, like teenagers, against the unnecessary conventions or ideas by which they feel constrained. They want to express themselves differently, often in a way alien to the existing norm. I remember how my parents felt about rock and roll. And how I felt.

Modern Art did not begin with Dada in 1915, but that is where I will start. Dadaism was a total revolt against existing art forms. Dada arose in Europe as a reaction to World War I and the nationalism that many thought had led to the war. The Dadaists were deliberately outrageous and disrespectful.

"Dada wished to replace the logical nonsense of men today with illogical nonsense," said the artist Francis Picabia's wife, Gabrielle. Marcel Duchamp submitted a urinal to an art exhibit and called it art. He introduced the mind into the consideration of art, not just the eye, and he turned the idea of what is art on its head. The idea itself could be art, not just the image. George Grosz declared "Art is dead," (which happens to be the title of my second art world mystery).

Dada faded rather quickly, and flowed into Surrealism, which explored the unconscious. This was the period when Dali painted his dripping clocks.

The 1940s and 1950s witnessed the rise of Abstract Expressionism. Firmly rooted in lower Manhattan, it was the first purely American modern art movement. Jackson Pollock and Mark Rothko sought to express emotion without form. Men dominated the movement.

Pollack painted huge, multicolored canvases by dripping, throwing and splattering paint on them in broad gestures. The paintings shouted emotion. Rothko, using what became Color Field techniques, painted shimmering, overlapping blocks of subtle color on untreated canvas. Robert Motherwell, Adolf Gottlieb, Willem de Kooning and Franz Kline were also noted artists of the time.

The Fluxus movement, which emerged in the 1950s, defined art in terms of experience as well as objects. The movement led to the art-as-performance world.

In the eighth New York Avant Garde Festival, John Lennon (of the Beatles) produced a piece of performance art where musicians played a musical piece as a rotating fan randomly shifted the pages of the sheet music. Geoffrey Hendricks, a leading Fluxus artist, stood on a mound of dirt that contained his wedding ring.

In the early 1960s, broad gestural painting morphed to include new modes of abstraction. Lyrical Abstract Expressionism, Color Field and Hard-Edged painting evolved. In this reflective and cerebral evolution, color took precedence over expressionistic surface texture.

Color Field painting, emphasizing hues and color, became more varied and intense. The Color Field artists thinned their paints, allowing them to soak into the canvas, creating intense luminosity. One of its leading figures, and one of the movement's few women, Helen Frankenthaler, became internationally famous.

Pop Art responded by focusing on the merger of art and commerce. The art was figurative, but the subject was commercial and blaring. Andy Warhol used popular culture and advertising images for his art, while Roy Lichtenstein used comic book-like figures and Ben-Day dots, which became his trademark. (Ben-Day dots are a printing process named after an illustrator and printer, Benjamin

Day. Depending on the effect, color or optical illusion needed, small colored dots are closely spaced, widely spaced, or overlapping.) The art was coolly ambivalent, in contrast to the hot emotions of the Abstract Expressionists or the romantic lyricism of Color Field.

Jasper John and Robert Rauschenberg were central forces in what became Pop Art. Rauschenberg's "Combines" used non-traditional materials and objects in new combinations. Johns used classic iconography to play with contradictions and paradoxes. His "Flag" paintings are among his best-known works.

Conceptualism traces its roots back to Marcel Duchamp's assertion that art was an idea and not just an image. It was founded on the principal that art is a concept and not a material object. The idea is central and the artifact is mere documentation.

By downplaying artistic skill, it created a subversive element and challenged the value of art objects. Important conceptual artists include Sol Lewitt, the father of conceptual art in the United States, Felix Gonzales-Torres and feminist Jenny Holzer, whose art focused on delivering words and ideas in public spaces.

Minimalism emerged in the mid-60s and was an answer to both the exuberance of Abstract Expressionism and the playful cynicism of Pop Art. It is characterized by an extreme simplicity and a deliberate lack of expressive content.

Minimalism dwelt on anonymous industrial manufacturing, such as the sculpture of Donald Judd. It is this simplicity that calls into question the nature of art and posits Minimalist sculpture as an object of contemplation. Or it is the line, color and form of Ellsworth Kelly. Minimalism sought a total absence of emotion in art, an austere purity.

Artists such as Judd created works comprising single or repeated geometric forms produced from industrialized, machine-made materials that eschewed the artist's touch. One of his famous sculptures is a set of monochromatic boxes, of uniform dimensions, rigorously spaced in line up a blank wall.

Kelly first rose to critical acclaim in the 1950's with his bright, multi-paneled and largely monochromatic canvases. Maintaining focus on the dynamic relationships between shape, form and color, his layered reliefs, flat sculptures, and line drawings challenged the conception of space. He presented bold and contrasting colors free of gestural brushstrokes or recognizable imagery, panels protruding gracefully from the wall, and irregular forms confidently inhabiting a space.

There is an important Kelly work on the side of the Hopkins Center for the Arts at Dartmouth College. It consists of five enormous rectangular wall panels, each of the same size, painted in a single block of color, yellow, green, blue, red and orange. A striking example of Minimalism.

It was so minimal, I found it hard to respond to. To say it didn't reach my soul is an understatement. In fact, I was surprised to learn it was a major work of art. I really should have known better given its placement and prominence.

Perhaps this was the perfect minimalist work. I like other examples of Kelly's work. But I need emotional involvement as the precondition to the art I like and it is exactly that which Minimalism seeks to deny. Is the minimalist work I respond to imperfect by definition?

On the other hand, as Anne and I were walking on campus, we came across a sculpture by Joel Shapiro. He is a sculptor who was new to me at the time, although he is quite well known. Shapiro crafts straight steel bars into human-like figures in various acts of motion. His work is distinctive. I would never have expected to be moved by the piece, but I was. I was confused. It was not a new condition for me.

In the later twentieth century some artists became disillusioned, feeling trapped by the need to make money. It was the artists' revolt against collectors and the perceived commercialization of their art. Collectors could determine if their work was good or bad, at least in terms of price. What did they know? How dare them. The artists rebelled.

Performance art is related to Conceptual Art, characterized by its "live" nature. This art sought to make itself ephemeral and therefore uncollectible. Performances were passing expressions of art. No one could own them (although the collectors did buy limited additions of recordings of the performances, as did museums). Christo went the other way, making art too large and impermanent to be collected.

He wrapped bridges and buildings with colorful material. Christo did sell plans and drawings to generate money to execute his vision.

This movement posed a challenge to museums, not in terms of their exhibition programing (they could mount a performance), but in terms of their permanent collections. How do you add something to your collection that only exists in time? Is a recording of it art? Is it the same art? How do you show it?

Now we are in the age of computer-generated and digital art. Artists are even experimenting with artificial intelligence that will produce its own art.

In October 2018, Christie's offered in New York the *Portrait of Edmond de Bellamy* (2018), an algorithm-created work. The algorithm responsible for the portrait was developed by a French art collective using a model called GAN (short for generative adversarial network). GAN can be trained to produce completely new, and dramatically different images. The estimate on the work was $7,000-$10,000. The picture sold for $432,500, 43 times its high estimate.

That raised some eyebrows. Carolyn Christov-Bakargiev, the curator of the Castello di Rivoli museum in Turin, observed that the conversation we should be having about AI concerns the historical relationship between technology, culture and humanity. "When you have the art market selling computer-made paintings. . .it's about investment. It's no longer about art."

Finally, there is Outsider Art, an area of art that is difficult to place chronologically since it has gone on forever. The name was derived from the term "Art Brut," originated by Jean Dubuffet in the 1940s to describe raw art, which he viewed as art created outside of official art culture.

The use of the term "Outsider Art" has been expanding over the years to refer to any artist who is untrained, disabled or suffering from exclusion. Outsider Art comes from the streets, from the poverty of rural America and from our asylums. Its power is in the raw emotion that permeates it. The naïve art of former slaves, an important aspect of Outsider Art, is becoming increasingly sought out and collectable. Works by Thornton Dial and Bill Traylor now command tens and hundreds of thousands of dollars.

Outsider Art has drawn a great deal of attention in the last few years with museum exhibitions, and dedicated auctions. Christie's, in January 2019, held an auction solely for Outsider and Vernacular Art. But the field is still fertile for exploration and discovery.

Street Art which, in its inception was Outsider Art, has emerged into an independent art genre that has become entrenched in the established art world. During the 1970s, graffiti art exploded across New York. Jean-Michael Basquiant was an untrained artist who sprayed graffiti on buildings but broke through as a solo artist in the early '80s. His aggressive and highly charged canvases screamed of street anger. He died of a heroin overdose at the age of 27 in 1988. In 2017 a painting by Basquiant sold at Sotheby's for $110.5 million, a new record high for any American artist.

There have been innumerable variations in art. Some have led to the question "What is art?" Some have led to the statement "My five-year-old child could do that." But, art doesn't go away. It is an endless and irresistible inquiry.

Chapter 23

# WHAT IS ART?

THIS IS AN AGE-OLD discussion. There are many views. But I don't think any of that is important. I assure you I will not resolve the question in this chapter.

Frankly, what others think is art is stimulating and may be informative. It may change our conclusions over time. But "What is art?" is a personal question.

I have an easier time with more traditional painting and sculpture, where technical artistic skill is evident, than with conceptual pieces where the idea is dominant. A painting may be good or bad. Is it so much like other art that it is derivative? Or poorly executed and amateurish (although a child-like perspective is a rare treasure many artists desire).

I don't believe there is a definitive answer. At least none I have discovered. And I have tried. But it is fun to ponder.

The visual stimulation of fine art is undeniable. But the mental stimulation is one of the joys of the art world. In art now, the idea is as important as the object. Maybe. There is one rule that I hold self-evident: I want to understand, I do not need to accept.

What is art?

I love to pose the question at our dinner parties. The discussion is always lively and rarely leads to physical violence.

Here is the question I ask. If I can produce a perfect copy of Van Gogh's *L'Etoile Nuit*, including the brush strokes and pigments, the aging, a copy so perfect no expert or technical test can distinguish it from the original, is that art? Most people say no.

Certainly, it is not *L'Etoile Nuit*. But it is. By definition, I can put the two pictures side by side and no one could tell the difference. "But it isn't an original idea," people say. But since the pictures are exactly the same, it gives the same joy as the original to someone looking at it who does not know it's a copy.

Well, the best answer I ever got was from a teacher of art history. She said art is whatever brings you an emotional response. So, the perfect duplicate is art. Only a different kind of art than the original. It wasn't a very satisfactory response to me. Something was missing.

What about Felix Gonzalez-Torres? He was a Cuban-born American artist. Openly gay, he was interested in the overlap of private and public life. He used everyday materials to address themes such as love and loss, asking the viewer to participate in his works. He died in 1996, at the age of 40. He was the subject of major museum exhibitions and his work is in many of the most important museum collections.

One of the most interesting examples of a modern conceptual work that I have seen was his candy spill work displayed at the Los Angeles Museum of Art. In the piece, 175 pounds (the prescribed "ideal" weight) of individually wrapped, commercial candy in multiple colors was spilled into a corner of the room, making a triangular mound.

Other spill pieces by Gonzalez-Torres take different forms (for example, a rectangle laid out on a floor) and the candy is of a different color (i.e., black licorice). The weight and shape of the spill are important.

Each installation has a different "ideal weight". It is the instruction to the museum on the weight of the candy to be spilled.

The "ideal weight" may relate to the subject of the spill.

But Gonzalez-Torres never explained the meaning. In the case of the spill I saw, it has been suggested that the 175 pounds was a tribute to the artist's partner who had died of AIDS (as did Gonzalez-Torres).

Each viewer was invited to take a piece of candy and consume it. At the end of each day, the museum staff topped up the spill.

The spill fascinated me because it was interactive. It drew the viewer in. There was a prize for viewing the art. The work focused attention and discussion, not the hurried walk-by of most art.

But underlying the effect was the intellectual thrust of the work

I was viewing. Each candy consumed was a part of his partner's wasting away. Each piece consumed was an interaction from which every one of us would shy away. (As I was correcting this sentence, I was reminded of Churchill's quote when asked what he thought of a dangling participle. He said, "This is the sort of pedantry up with which I will not put.") In a broader sense perhaps, it was the cycle of life, diminishing and renewing.

One of the Gonzalez Torres's spill works sold at Christie's in 2015 for $7.7 million. There was an elaborate system in place for the owner to prove it was original so the piece could be re-sold. A certificate of authenticity and specific instructions were issued by the Gonzalez-Torres Foundation and photo documentation was provided with the work.

I would say the price was jaw dropping. But I wouldn't say that because you would think I was reaching for a pun.

It was conceptual because the art lay primarily in the idea. The work did not reflect the craftwork of the artist.

A work of art may be understood as a bridge from the artist's mind to the viewer's. This was commercial candy. It was not even the same candy with which the work was originally created because it was renewed nightly by the museum staff. The "ideal weight" could not be exactly retained from minute to minute or day to day. What if the same brand of candy was not available?

Is this art? I think so. It certainly fulfilled my tests. It was intended as art (which I think is critical). It engaged me emotionally and it made me think.

John Baldisseri is a wonderful artist whom I have admired for many years. He is respected and broadly collected in the museum community.

He has a work in the Broad Museum in Los Angeles entitled "Tips For Artists Who Want to Sell" that he executed between 1966 and 1968. He found the "tips" in a magazine and tore them out. He then sent the page to a commercial sign painter with instructions to paint the words in black on a plain, flat yellow surface. He did not supervise the production, did not put his hand to the work, but when it was completed he took delivery and signed it.

The painted words are:

- Generally speaking paintings with light colors sell more quickly than paintings with dark colors.

- Subjects that sell well:

  Madonna and child, Landscapes, Flower paintings, Still Lifes ( Free of Morbid Props___Dead birds, etc.), nudes, Marine Pictures, Abstracts and Surrealism.

- Subject Matter is Important: It has Been said that paintings with cows and hens in them collect dust___While the same paintings with Bulls and roosters sell.

Now this painting at first confounded me. After all, the presentation of someone else's product as art goes back 100 years to when Marcel Duchamp put forth his urinal. Why repeat the idea?

Why did Eli Broad buy it? You don't even want to know the price. What was new here?

Neither Baldisseri nor Broad would talk to me, although I didn't ask them. But here is the explanation given by Baldessari:

"There is a certain kind of work one could do that didn't require a studio. It's work that is done in one's head. The artists could be the facilitator of the work; executing it (is) another matter." Baldessari was one of the key artists in the development of Conceptual Art.

This thought that an artist could present an idea rather than a material object from his or her own hand was a way for Baldessari to reassert the notion of what art could be. In 1966, art meant mostly painting, sculpture, drawing or printmaking. Baldessari challenged this expectation. Besides, he did it with a sense of humor.

To me, Baldisseri was doing something that went beyond what had gone before, and that is what made it an interesting painting. He seemed to me to be commenting on the increasing commercialism of artists in the art world, and the absurdity surrounding art. I think he was also mocking the use of others to do the work. If you would, the corporatization of art. For me at least, this created a new internal discussion, and that is art.

Sol Lewitt, a great conceptual artist as well as renowned Minimalist said, "Ideas alone can be works of art. All ideas need not be made physical... It may never leave the artist's mind." The thought that art can be an unexpressed idea certainly presents a new challenge. My mind reels and boggles at the thought. But my thought isn't art.

Obviously, it is difficult to determine what is conceptual art if everything an artist does in his or her studio is art. But what if everything an artist does anywhere is art?

Valerie Solanas was a fringe figure in the circle of Andy Warhol's Factory. On June 3, 1968, she shot Warhol three times. He was only given a 50-50 chance of surviving. After two months in the hospital, Warhol returned to the Factory. He was still a Pop Art star, but he wasn't doing the work. That had gone on in his absence. After all, that was the idea of the Factory.

But Warhol was confused. "I knew the work was going on, even if I didn't have any idea what the work would come to," he said. Then he realized it. The corporate work was some of his most important art. The business is art, the step that comes after art.

Blake Gopnik, in *The New York Times* said, "The heart of Warhol's idea—that by playing the role of businessman, an artist could turn himself into the latest living example of a commodification he believed none of us can avoid was perhaps as revolutionary... as Marcel Duchamp's... declaration that artists alone get to define what is art." So, everything that Warhol did to pursue his business was itself art.

Really? I have trouble with the concept. It seems like more of an excuse to me than an idea. And Warhol had a deep sense of cynicism.

But the writer and curator Jack Bankowsky said, "Business Art remains as important as it ever was, because Andy Warhol is as important as he ever was." And important he still is. In November 2018, the Whitney opened its major new survey of Warhol's art, "Andy Warhol—From A to B and Back Again."

Of course, conceptual art can lend itself to abuse. I don't have to be much of an artist to hang an empty picture frame on the wall and call it *The World in the Absence of Art* (which I did in one of my art world mystery novels). But how about nailing a piece of rope to a board or painting a canvas pure white (both of which are actual examples by respected artists; the white piece inspired the play *Art*).

Peter Schjeldahl, the art critic for *The New Yorker*, reviewed the sprawling retrospective at MoMA of the work of Bruce Nauman (1941-). Nauman is a renowned conceptual artist. He studied mathematics, physics and music theory at the University of Wisconsin but discovered contemporary art on visits to Chicago. In 1964, he rose to art world fame as a defining force in Conceptualism.

Nauman burst upon the New York scene in 1968 at his debut at Leo Castelli's. Castelli was a legendary dealer in the art world. He represented Robert Rauschenberg and introduced Jasper Johns.

There Nauman established himself as a deeply intellectual artist who was antagonistic to commercial culture and indifferent to judgements of taste. He believed, along with Sol Lewitt, that anything an artist does in the artist's studio must be art. He made monotonous video tapes, repeating random motions or repeated routines, bringing the droning passage of real time into the isolation of the exhibit space.

He felt that a work only had to be finished to the point where it embodied its ideas. So, many of his works seem crude. Critics reacted with horror and disgust. Schjeldahl notes that many Nauman works are often an ordeal for the viewer.

Schjeldahl admits that he had trouble with Nauman's work when he first saw it. Nauman does not beguile. But he was clearly serious and disciplined.

During his interview with Schjeldahl, Nauman coaxed Schjedahl into riding with him. He says about Nauman's art, "I became, like one of his horses, broken into a decision to like his work, as an option less difficult than making a decision to dislike it. Decision is necessary."

Such pieces always lead to the statement: "My five-year-old child could do that." Yes, but that isn't the point, even if your child could, or actually did it. There is an intellectual foundation to conceptual art. You need to examine the idea, whether you agree with it or not. Of course, you can still reject it as a piece as art. And you don't have to buy it.

When I was a kid, I liked Mogen David. Now I think an '82 Mouton Rothschild is better. It took me a long time to get from there to here. Art in that sense is like wine. The more you look, the more you study, the more you know, the richer the experience of deciding for yourself "What is art?"

# Chapter 24

# Mistakes

WE ALL MAKE MISTAKES. No matter how thorough and careful we are. If you are really clever, you will never make the same mistake twice. You will find a new way to err. I am really clever.

I bought a 4-inch metal sculpture by Tom Holland. When it came, it was a 4-foot sculpture. It was a misprint. Ooops! Fortunately, I had a good place for it outside. And I probably got a bargain because no one else bid on it. Who wants a 4-inch sculpture?

And then there was the Joe Goode piece. It was from his Midnight series. The work on paper was all black and folded in places. It had cut outs. I think I was influenced by my desire to have a Joe Goode work in our collection. I admire his art. The piece had a really great signature (laugh here).

I never liked the piece after I hung it. It was too dark. It just didn't pop. I couldn't get the lighting right.

It is one of the problems in buying art without looking at it on a wall. But even if you look at it on the wall of a gallery or in an auction house, it will look different when you put it on your wall. Their space is more open and they have professional lighting.

I was lucky. I sold it after 2 years for enough money, after the seller's commission, to recoup all of my original dollars. I may have actually made $20.

I own a John Chamberlin print. It was in an edition of only 6, which is very small. But Chamberlin is known primarily for his crushed metal sculptures. The print was nice, but it didn't ring my chimes after a while. I will sell it. Be careful about buying a piece outside of the artist's main genre.

A tale: I had purchased a wonderful bronze statue called *The Bather* from a Seattle sculptor, Joseph McDonnell. As I mentioned, I collect dead artists, but live sculptors. I know that is irrational. But I find it helps if you need to communicate with the sculptor.

Bronze sculptures are cast in series. This one was number three in a series of up to eight. When the sculpture had been cast, Joe called me. The sculpture was an outdoor piece, about three feet high. I didn't think it was big enough to sit on the ground.

I asked Joe if he was going to make me a plinth, a base. He said he could, but he had always imagined this sculpture sitting on a basalt column. As it turns out, basalt is granite that appears sometimes in columnar form. But he was emphatic that the base had to be exactly 22" tall. I take instructions well, particularly if they are simple.

I immediately went down to my local stone yard. I don't live in a large town, so my local stone yard is rather small. I really didn't expect much. I wandered around, but low and behold, there was the perfect basalt column. Only it was 37" tall.

I went into the office and told the clerk behind the counter that I wanted the basalt column, but it had to be cut to 22". He nodded slowly, and then he explained that basalt was a very dense material. It would cost as much to cut the stone as to purchase it.

Now this is the part where a superior education plays an important role in art. "Why don't you just dig a 15" hole in the ground," he asked. I still have a flat spot on my forehead from pounding my head on the desk. The sculpture looks great.

And I have a simply grand glass sculpture by Michael Pavlik, a renowned Czech glass artist. It was one of my first purchases at the Santa Monica Art Auction. I absolutely loved the piece, a geometric series of glass planes with a red glass ball resting on top. But it had a chip in one of the glass planes. I bought it anyway.

The damage bothered me over time. I tried to consult Pavlik, but I couldn't find him. I took the sculpture to the best glass art restorer in the Western United States. We talked about all kinds of possibilities including beveling the piece to eliminate the chip, cutting out an area including the chip or filling in the chip with clear epoxy. We decided on the latter. The other alternatives would change the work. That seemed wrong.

Epoxy is clear, but it doesn't look like glass. I now have the sculpture turned so the epoxied area is not visible. It is better than it was before, but I still know the chip is there and I cringe when anyone looks closely at the piece in fear they might notice. Even though I still love the piece and I bought it at a great price because of the chip, I don't think I would buy it today.

Much later, a Dan Christensen acrylic on canvas came up for auction. We really like Christensen, and the piece was from the same series as two acrylics on paper by Christensen that we own. He is the only artist represented in our collection by more than one piece.

We wanted it. But it had a two-inch water spot on the unpainted portion of the canvas.

Learning from my debacle with the Pavlik, I called the restorers I use in Santa Barbara. They are quite good. I was referred to them by an art professor at Westmont College. The Santa Barbara Museum of Art uses them for its restoration projects.

We obviously did not yet own the piece. That complicated the process. I sent them the image (enlargeable) that the auction house provided at my request. The restorers believed that the canvas could be cleaned, although they were careful to make no promises.

They also quoted me, reluctantly, a guess on the cost. We needed that to figure out what to bid. They thought the restoration would cost around $1,000. And obviously, there was risk involved. They hadn't promised restoration and the cost was only an estimate. Even if the estimate was correct, if the work could not be restored, we still would have to pay for the effort and we would have a more expensive damaged work on our hands.

We decided to take the risk, hoping that the damage would put off other bidders and that we could get the piece at a price that would absorb the cost of restoration and the risk. We bid on the lot and won the work. The restorers did wonders at the estimated cost. We enjoy the piece every day. We got lucky.

Finally, there is the Gechtoff work on paper, our great triumph, for which I broke my arm patting myself on the back.

The piece is large, around 4-feet by 5-feet. But we had the wall for it. I and my trusty tape measure were certain. We won the bid for $1,625, all in. We were full of joy.

That is until the shipper told me it would cost $960 to ship. I had checked the cost of shipping before bidding. It was around $400. But what neither the shipper nor I knew was that the dimensions of the piece did not include the frame.

That posed two problems: Was our bargain not such a bargain? Oh, I know. We are only talking about $2,600. It was not the end of the world. But, for me, things are relative and it raised the cost by 65%.

However, there was a more important problem: I had little margin for error on the wall where the picture was to hang. And a wife who would not be happy with a picture leaning up against the wall instead of hanging on it.

The shipper and I put our heads together. I had done business with them before and they pitched in. They could ship the piece for $400 if they took it out of the frame and shipped it flat. And it would be only $150 if they rolled it up and put it in a tube.

I have a frugal nature. Things must meet a value standard in my head. But even I didn't want to risk having the picture rolled up to save $250, though the risk was small. So, I was looking at an unframed picture for $400.

I called my framer. He could frame the piece for $600. And the frame could be thin enough to fit our wall. It still cost me a $1000 to get the picture here and get it framed. Both problems solved, but I was a little sobered by the experience. That is not the best of states for someone who really likes wine.

I love looking at our Gechtoff in its new frame. It sits in a place of pride at the end of our entry hallway.

I will never make that mistake again. I will find a new one to make.

# Chapter 25
## OWNING ART

IF YOU COLLECT ART, display and lighting are central to your enjoyment. The picture must be placed at the correct height, in the right place and centered properly on the wall. Maybe you're good at this. I'm not.

Professionals can be costly. We like to use professionals in their time off. It saves money. After all, these professionals are putting extra money in their pockets, with no overhead.

There are two ways I have found of securing such help. Both ways have produced excellent people.

Look at the college extension catalog from the community college in your area. There will be numerous art courses. See if one of the professors fits your needs. Even if s/he doesn't, s/he is likely to be able to recommend a colleague.

Or see if such a person works at the local museum or at a university museum. Even small museums have people dedicated to mounting exhibits and lighting art. The art world does not pay well. There are always people who are highly qualified who are doing the job because they love it. They are trained and would be grateful to make some extra money. And many people in the art world, particularly among the academics and museum folk, are nice and very intelligent.

We have been using a young professor from a small college museum for years. He is knowledgeable and enthusiastic. His work is impeccable. And he has been able to recommend other professionals of the highest quality for restoration and framing.

Do not underestimate the impact of lighting on your art. The piece presents differently in different lighting. And the colors change remarkably.

Also, be aware of the effect of sunlight on your art. Particularly with watercolors and prints, infrared light leeches color over time. It can do severe damage and ruin the work. Have your pictures framed with UV protective glass or plastic. If you have a problem with reflection, museum glass reduces glare, although it is more expensive.

You also need to be handy with a tape measure, both to determine where you can put a piece of art and the size of the piece you are considering bidding on. Even I can do this.

---

One drawback of looking at art in a catalog and purchasing online is that all the images are the same size. Size makes a great difference, and it is easy to overlook or misjudge. A 7-inch x 10-inch picture presents in a completely different way than a 20-inch x 20-inch art work. A piece that blows you away in the image may be unimpressive on your wall.

In Sotheby's auctions, they have added a feature. They provide a picture of a person standing in front of a wall with the auction lot. It is enormously helpful in visualizing the art work. If no image is provided, you have to get out your trusty tape measure and recreate the size for yourself. Use sheets of 8-inch by 10-inch paper taped together to recreate the size of the piece. It is really useful in visualizing the impact of the art.

Before you bid, figure out where you will hang the piece. Wall space limitations frustrate all collectors. An art collection is like a jigsaw puzzle. You can spend hours trying to figure out how to move your art to accommodate a new piece. Then you have to convince your spouse.

Every collector runs out of wall space. Some collectors pack their walls with art, hanging picture above picture. Salon style, as opposed to a more spacious presentation, is hanging pictures densely on the wall, one above another and side by side. It speaks of art at the expense of the unique quality of each work. It is difficult to focus on a single work. But, with little wall space and a passion for art, it works. Some collectors even have art stacked against the walls or in special storage areas.

We prefer a display like we often see in museums, with the art spaced well apart. But that presents us with a constant dilemma of where to put new art. I know every unutilized space in our house. I have measured each of them.

I have also made a list of pieces I want to consider selling or donating in order to upgrade our collection. I have asked Anne to give me a list of her six least-favorite works. It is not easy. It is like selling the children. And besides, you may not agree. Let me modify that. You will not agree.

The good news is that if you run out of wall space and have no art you do not love completely, you can always collect sculpture. It looks great on the lawn.

There is the thrill of the hunt, but the thrill of owning great art is different. Needless to say, like all good things, you can overdo it. It is easy for a passion to become an obsession. A collection can become a clutter, no matter how great the art. You can't appreciate it if it overwhelms you.

I remember seeing a documentary about Alan Stone. Stone was a passionate collector who became a dealer. He discovered Wayne Thiebaud.

Thiebaud paints commonplace subjects in a figurative manner, with a psychological twist. It is remarkable art but was out of step with many other kinds of contemporary art.

Thiebaud was unknown and unrepresented. He kept pestering Stone until Stone took some of his work on spec. When Stone hung them on the wall with some important artists, he noted, over time, that they held their own on the wall, perhaps the best way to test any art work. Thiebaud became a hot artist through the quality of his art and Stone's efforts.

Eventually, Stone gave up the gallery and retreated to his large house. There were so many pieces of art in his house, and so many other collections that there was no wall space or shelf space. And no floor space.

Literally, no space. You had to turn sideways to walk through the rooms. No matter how much he loved art, for me, that overdid it. I left the theatre with a feeling of claustrophobia. I can still feel the pressure on my chest as I write this.

# Chapter 26

## CATALOGING AND INSURANCE

KEEP A LOOSE-LEAF BOOK of your art. Make two copies and keep one away from the house, but close by so you can update it. I keep my second copy in the trunk of my car. The second copy will be helpful if your house burns down. Mine did.

Make a copy of the lot page from the auction catalog and slip it into a three-punched plastic sleeve. The lot page will give you a picture of the art, its dimensions, the material from which it is made, the estimated value and often the condition. It will also tell you where and when you bought it.

Behind it, in the same sleeve, facing the other way, put *The New York Times* obituary or other research on the artist and particularly include the museum collections in which the artist is represented. In the middle put the invoice from the auction house and note the other expenses, like shipping.

Your book will be a wonderful resource. You can find the name of the artist when you forget it. The older you get, the more you forget. It will also be a terrific reference in discussing your collection with others.

At some point, you will want to get your art insured. The insurer will require that your art be appraised. This binder will be very helpful to the appraiser.

Insurance is cheap. The most expensive part, at least up-front, is the cost of the appraiser. Make sure your appraiser is a certified fine art appraiser and acceptable to the insurance company. He or she should belong to the American Society of Appraisers.

A qualified appraiser will cost $100 an hour or more. He or she will come to your home and examine and photograph each piece. The appraiser will then seek comparative pieces in the marketplace and value each work. You will receive a written report on the insurance value of your collection, by piece, with a summary letter. Send the report to the insurance company. The insurance company will then annoy you with requests you never thought about. Give them what they need.

"Insurance value" is a different concept than "fair market value," although the two are obviously related. Fair market value is the price at which an object will change hands between a willing buyer and a willing seller. It is based on comparable sales at a contemporary time. It includes the costs of the transaction, in this case the buyer's premium. This value is what you need for the IRS to deduct a donation of art.

Insurance value is different. It is the highest amount that would be required to replace the object with objects of similar quality, condition and provenance. The insurance value, in many cases is significantly higher than fair market value. So, when you hear an expert on *Antiques Road Show* giving an insurance value to a work, take it with a grain of salt.

My appraisal cost me four times the annual cost of the insurance, so it takes a while to amortize the cost. Keep the insurance for a long time.

# Chapter 27

## TALES FROM THE JUNGLE

WHERE LOTS OF MONEY flows, bad people follow right along. The art world is an unregulated jungle. Forgery, fraud and breach of fiduciary duty are its hazards, along with simple omissions or outright lies.

The provenance (history of ownership) of a piece of art is important for several reasons. You need to ascertain that the painting is real, not a forgery or a copy.

Christie's was sued by a buyer who had purchased a Sisley oil for around $350,000 a decade before. A third party claimed the work had been looted by the Nazis and the seller did not have good title. The third party, asserting he was the rightful owner, was now seeking the return of the art.

Christie's claimed it was not negligent in its examination of the provenance of the painting. They could not have reasonably discovered the defect in title as a result of Nazi looting. They had used reasonable diligence. The computerization of looted art ownership had advanced dramatically since the time of the sale, they claimed. No matter who won, the buyer lost. It cost a lot of money to make the claim. And a lot of emotional distress.

More importantly, if the piece has passed through the hands of a major gallery, you can be certain, at least at that time, the artist was well regarded. If the piece was previously sold at auction, you can ascertain the price the piece was sold for and the time it remained in the hands of the buyer. If it was sold quickly, it raises a concern that you need to address. Is there something wrong with the work?

While forgery usually is not a real worry, except at the upper levels of collecting (after all, who wants to forge a $5,000 painting although there have been some forgery issues involving Outsider artists), every collector should understand the problem. Forgery is endemic in the art world. Thomas Hoving, the former director of the Metropolitan Museum, said, "In the decade (1967-1977) that I was with the Metropolitan Museum of Art, I must have examined 50,000 works of art. Fully 40% per cent were either phonies or so hypocritically restored or so misattributed that they were just the same as forgeries. Since then I'm sure that percentage has risen."

*The Independent* of London stated "A reasonable estimate might be that at least 20 per cent of the paintings held by our major (UK) museums, some up on the walls, many others in the vaults, will no longer be attributed to the same painter 100 years from now."

These quotes may be an overstatement, and they deal with misattribution as well as forgery. But a specialty museum in France just discovered that over half of its art was forged. It was stunned.

The CBS-TV news-magazine series *60 Minutes* had a major expose on a forger who did not copy art but painted in the style of the artist he was forging. He was quite good. This forger painted abstract works because they were easier to forge than Old Masters or Impressionists (although there are numerous books on forgers who successfully forged both).

He proudly asserted his art was hanging in many major museums. His criminal activity was not discovered for a score of years, and then only because he became careless with a tube of paint that contained a chemical element unavailable at the time the forged artist lived.

Johannes Vermeer, the Dutch Golden Age painter of the 1660s, is a master, widely admired for his poetic manner. There are just 34, perhaps 35, paintings firmly attributed to him (together with six paintings referenced in the historical records and lost). In 1866, there were 74. Vermeer is one of the most forged of the old masters. As his reputation grew in the twentieth century, many of the forgeries were identified.

But as the number of identified forgeries dwindled, the supply also grew. Perhaps the best known of the forgers was Han Van Meegeren.

His forgeries were awkward, but he learned to give his paintings age by dying them in the oven and then adding craquelure (the cracked surface that emerges as the oil paint dries) by rolling them over his knee.

Van Meegeren became famous for selling one of his Vermeers to Hermann Goering. Goering was anxious to acquire one for his collection. Goering was noted for his insatiable desire for art and had a special Nazi unit that was responsible for looting on his behalf. You have to admit, selling a fake to the German high command was a gutsy move.

But after the liberation, Van Meegeren was arrested for trading with the enemy and put on trial. He confronted a real Hobson's choice (not a Morton's fork). In his defense, he claimed that he had given Goering nothing of value, it was a forgery (which, of course, was in itself a crime, but a far less serious one).

To prove his point, he painted another "Vermeer" on the spot as the press and the public looked on. He died a Dutch hero as the man who swindled Goering.

New art works are discovered all the time. In December 2015, while helping an elderly neighbor in Arizona move into a retirement home, a local man spotted a signed Los Angeles Lakers poster in the garage. He contacted an appraiser believing the poster could be valuable. Employees of the appraiser, while sorting through the junk, discovered a group of paintings that appeared to be by Jackson Pollock, Kenneth Noland, Jules Olitski and others.

The homeowner had inherited the paintings from his half-sister many years before. He never paid much attention to them. Investigators determined that the sister, a New York socialite, had been friends with both Clement Greenberg, the eminent art critic and essayist, and with the sister of socialite and arts philanthropist, Peggy Guggenheim. They were friends with the artists whose works were found in the garage. It explained how his sister had the paintings and helped to establish their authenticity.

There are numerous examples of art being found in barns or attics in the United States and Europe. When the picture was created, the artist wasn't important. The painting was sold, hopefully, but might have been given away or traded for food or lodging. In many cases, at the time, the art was not worth the canvas on which it was painted. The trade was an act of kindness.

Artists moved. They died. They got divorced or sick. There were wars. There were fires. Art was destroyed or looted. The art got shunted aside or moved to some closet or cellar. It was ugly.

That is why it is still possible to discover rare and valuable art. Or to forge it and claim to have found it.

The part of the jungle we play in is usually too unprofitable to attract the unethical, immoral or criminal element. But, it is both interesting and fun to spend some time among the scoundrels, schemes and scams. Who knows, it might even be useful.

A diminutive, dapper man with twinkling blue eyes named Frank Lloyd built the Marlborough Gallery in London into the wealthiest, most important art gallery business in the world in the mid-twentieth century. Marlborough was Francis Bacon's sole dealer.

Marlborough agreed, in 1958, to acquire all of Bacon's paintings (other than those Bacon destroyed; a small problem he had. Marlborough gave Bacon an assistant, part of whose job was to get the paintings out of his studio quickly).

Marlborough paid Bacon a set price per painting (without an inflation index or price increases during the term), based solely on size. Say, $600 for a 20" x 24" oil. The agreement lasted for 34 years, from 1958 until 1992, when Bacon died.

In the final 10 years of the agreement, Bacon received from Marlborough a total of $375,000. In 1983, near the start of the final decade of the contract, the gallery sold a single work for $250,000.

Following Bacon's death, his estate sued Marlborough for fraud, undue influence and missing art. Marlborough disputed the claims and defended its actions, saying it was not Bacon's agent and owed him no fiduciary duty. Marlborough was a purchaser. It was just a business deal.

Nine years later, the estate abandoned its law suit. It stated that its sole beneficiary was terminally ill. There were no further beneficiaries. All claims were dismissed.

There is another story about Marlborough. It is perhaps related. Its

New York gallery opened in 1963 on East 57th Street after making a nearly clean sweep of the most important Abstract Expressionists, representing Robert Motherwell, Mark Rothko, and Adolph Gottlieb and the estates of Jackson Pollock and Franz Kline.

When Mark Rothko committed suicide in 1970, he left behind 798 paintings on canvas and paper. In November 1971, the artist's daughter went to court to have the three executors of her father's estate removed and the contract they had signed with Marlborough nullified.

The executors had contracted with Marlborough to acquire 100 Rothko paintings for $1.8 million ($18,000 each), payable in 12 years without interest. And the executors further agreed to the consignment of the remaining 698 works for a period of 12 years at a sales commission of 40 to 50 percent.

The executors were Bernard J. Reis, who was also Marlborough's chief accountant, Theodoros Stamos, an artist represented by the gallery, and Morton Levine, a professor of anthropology. All had been close friends of Rothko.

After an eight-month trial, the court-imposed damages and fines totaling $9.2 million against the executors, Marlborough's Frank Lloyd and his gallery and canceled the contract with Marlborough. The conduct of the executors was judged "manifestly wrongful and indeed shocking."

In 1983, Mr. Lloyd was convicted of tampering with evidence in the trial. Theodoros Stamos was shunned by the art world and eventually returned to Greece.

## Chapter 28
## More Tales

FORGERY IS A DIFFERENT ANIMAL roaming the art jungle. The Knoedler scandal shook the art world by the ease with which a major fraud could be perpetrated. Knoedler was an esteemed gallery. It was the oldest continuous gallery in the United States.

In mid-1990s, a trusted and treasured employee introduced the President of Knoedler to "a very good friend," Glafira Rosales, a small art dealer and Carlos Bergantinos, her live-in companion.

Bergantinos had previously met a struggling, talented and obscure artist, Pei-Shen Qian, who had fled Communist China for Queens. Qian desperately needed money, even a few dollars. Bergantinos offered him $200 to imitate the work of a modern master. He liked what he saw.

Berganitos followed with dozens of additional projects to paint Pollacks, Rothkos and Klines. He scoured flea markets and garage sales for old canvas, Masonite and boards. He sought out old paints.

Berganitos stained the finished paintings with tea leaves and left them out in the elements to age them. Someone forged the artists names at the bottom of the canvas.

But the paintings needed provenance. Glafira Rosales created the back-story. Purportedly, a renowned (and now deceased) dealer had steered his closet lover to the studios of the masters of Abstract Expressionism and the lover purchased dozens of their works over time. The deals were always made for cash and there were no receipts because the artists did not want to pay taxes. The part about the cash was very believable.

Rosales produced a letter stating she represented the sellers, descendants of the closet lover, who desired to remain anonymous. It was not an unusual request. They resided in Switzerland and Mexico. The letter asserted they had acquired the art by inheritance.

Rosales approached the President of Knoedler, with whom she had developed a solid relationship. Even though Knoedler had previously had issues with the authenticity of two Diebenkorns they had purchased through Rosales, the opportunity to acquire this trove of treasures was too great. Notwithstanding the sketchy provenance, Knoedler agreed to sell the paintings.

The first painting Knoedler sold was a Pollack. The purchaser submitted it to an expert who found the provenance improbable and the painting questionable. The Buyer returned the painting to Knoedler and received a refund.

But Knoedler's relationship with Rosales continued. Knoedler sold a Rothko to a buyer for $8.3 million. The buyer stated he was told by Knoedler that the painting had been authenticated by Rothko's son and that Knoedler personally knew the seller.

The resulting lawsuit ultimately led to decimated careers, criminal indictments and the closing of Knoedler. Rosales pleaded guilty to criminal charges after the F.B.I. discovered other forgeries in the studio of the Chinese artist who had fled the United States.

There was a residual case resulting from the sale of another Rothko by Knoedler in 2008, this one for only $7.2 million. The purchaser, Frank J. Fertitta, sued the Swiss art expert, Oliver Wick, whom he accused of aiding in the fraud. The complaint alleged the "willful blindness or reckless disregard of the truth" by Mr. Wick.

Mr. Wick had been, at the time, a curator at the Beyeler Foundation, which had included the fake Rothko in an exhibition. He was paid a fee by Knoedler and confirmed in writing that ". . . all is perfectly fine (with the work). For this I stand with my name as a Rothko scholar."

Mr. Wick contended that he had assumed the work was genuine and not vouched for it personally. And that, in any case, he was not a party to the contract with Mr. Fertitta. Mr. Wick won the parallel case filed in Switzerland and, according to his lawyer, David Bran, "was cleared of any wrong doing." Perhaps.

Even so, think of the costs involved in that defense. Opinions of authenticity are becoming more difficult and more expensive to obtain. Artist's foundations are rejecting requests for authentication. The legal exposure of an expert is enormous and the seller may not be around to defend a lawsuit against him, even if it is obligated to do so by a contract of indemnification.

Ely Sakhai was a well-regarded art dealer who had another twist on forgery. In the 1980s he purchased several great paintings by Chagall, Gaugin, Monet and Klee. He took the original certificates of authenticity, and over a period of time, sold high quality forgeries of the works to Japanese collectors in a series of private sales.

After a few years, he sold the originals, applying for and receiving new certificates of authenticity claiming the originals were lost or destroyed. After all, he had the original paintings and clear proof of title.

His scheme came crashing down in May of 2000 when it was discovered that a Japanese seller was offering Paul Gauguin's *Vase de Fleurs (Lilas)* through Christie's when Sakhai was selling the same Gauguin through Sotheby's. Really, really bad timing.

The paintings were pulled from both auctions. They were submitted to Sylvie Crussard, a Gauguin expert, who had no trouble identifying the original. The forgery was excellent, but when placed side by side, one looked old and the other looked new, despite Sakhai's best efforts to artificially age his fake.

The fake was finally traced back to Sakhai by the FBI. Sakhai pleaded guilty to fraud. It is estimated he made $25 million from his scheme, when $25 million was a lot of money.

Jasper Johns was ripped off by his trusted foundry which was hired to make a mold of his original sculpted metal "Flag", in order to cast additional works. The foundry never returned the mold, although it was requested to do so on numerous occasions. There was always some excuse. The foundry cast and sold additional "Flag"s to collectors, claiming they were gifts from Johns.

Lisa Jacobs worked as an art advisor and part-time curator to

Hannelore Schulhof for 14 years. In October of 2011, shortly before Schulhof died, Jacobs agreed in writing to sell a Basquiat painting owned by Schulhof for not less than $6 million. She was to receive a 4% commission. The agreement specified Jacobs was not to accept any fee from the purchaser.

She found a purchaser for $6.5 million. She told the executor of Schulhof's estate that she had a firm offer for $5.5, non-negotiable. The buyer wanted to remain anonymous. The offer was accepted.

To preserve the buyer's secrecy, Jacobs suggested using a back-to-back escrow arrangement, where the painting would be sold to her and she would sell it to the buyer. When the escrows closed, she received a check for $6.5 million and forwarded $5.45 million, the alleged purchase price, less her commission to the estate.

In August of 2017, the court decided Jacobs was an agent as a matter of contract and had a fiduciary obligation to the seller. The court awarded the estate $1.55 million, without costs.

The lawsuit was filed in 2014. It took three years to resolve the case, even though it was decided on Summary Judgement and never went to trial. Incidentally, Jacobs had countersued the executor for sexual harassment.

Art frauds are difficult to find and difficult to prove. Most art frauds are dealt with in civil court, which is both expensive and time consuming. And even if a plaintiff prevails, he or she still has to find someone from whom to collect. Companies go bankrupt, people move overseas. Assets are transferred or hidden away.

The most common complaint, according to the New York Police Department, is "consignment fraud." That is one we all have to worry about. It is so common, it is hard to pick an example.

It occurs when a painting is consigned to a dealer who sells it and "forgets" to forward the proceeds. If questioned, he will have all manner of excuses and nothing ever seems to happen. Eventually, if the consignor persists, the dealer may be prosecuted, but sending a crook to jail doesn't get your money back.

Even a collector as sophisticated as Michael Ovitz can be taken. Ovitz has a 28,000 square foot house in Beverly Hills. It has three interconnected blocks, wrapped in a perforated steel skin. The house was constructed for his art. And his art is breathtaking.

His entryway is filled with Kellys, Judds, Shapiros and Lewitts. He has a small den where three Picasso oils reside comfortably with a Jean Arp maquette. His large dining room is dominated by a major Rothko painting, hung beside a Kline oil, with a beautiful Gottlieb next to it.

Michael doesn't invite us over for dinner often now (well, actually, he never did), but it would be an experience to sit at his artist-made dining room table, with museum-quality art over your shoulder, looking across the room at a wall-sized black Louise Nevelson. To your right, if you should happen to glance at the lawn, is a monumental Dubuffet sculpture from his Hourloupe series, one of Ovitz's two Dubuffets.

Down the stairs is his collection of works by living artists. Like many museums, a large part of this contemporary collection is stored and occasionally rotated. He has two full time curators. The security of his home, both electronic and human, is worthy of a major museum. Michael Ovitz is a sophisticated collector.

In 2013, he placed two Richard Prince pieces on consignment with the Perry Rubenstein Gallery. Ovitz's lawsuit alleged that Rubenstein sold one for $475,000, without his permission and below the agreed upon $575,000 minimum price, then did not turn over the proceeds.

Ovitz also alleged that Rubenstein agreed to sell the other Prince to a Mexican buyer for $500,000 but told Ovitz the Mexican buyer was slow in paying. When Ovitz demanded return of the work, the art was not forthcoming. The Rubenstein Gallery filed for bankruptcy in 2014.

In March of 2016, Rubenstein reached a settlement with Ovitz pursuant to which he returned one of the Princes. Rubenstein was arrested one month later. He pleaded no contest to the two counts of grand theft by embezzlement and in 2017 was sentenced to serve a six-month jail term and required to pay restitution. It is expected that only a small fraction of the ordered restitution will be paid.

# Chapter 29

# A Final Word

Two points.

First, art collectors are passionate about their art. That is what this whole book has been about. They love to talk about art and show their collection. They believe they know much more about art than anyone who doesn't collect. And they know much more about their collection than anyone who does.

If you notice that someone to whom you are speaking has a blank stare and perhaps is drooling from the side of his mouth, you have exceeded his interest. Find another collector to talk to.

Second, if you get infected with the passion of collecting and the excitement of the hunt and you love each object you acquire, I have a recommendation: Think about giving your son or daughter a piece of art to hang in their home. Let them pick the piece. Or offer to fund the purchase of a piece for them.

My son came up to visit and brought my 16-year old granddaughter. I was really chuffed when she asked me to show her our art. We went through the collection and she seemed very interested.

We gifted her a small piece for her birthday. Not to be outdone, her brother asked for his own piece to hang in his room. That may be the real joy of collecting.

So, give your granddaughter a piece of art for her dorm room. She will be grateful. She may even learn to love it. Maybe you can plant a seed that will blossom and enrich her life. You can afford it. You bought great art on a shoestring.

# Acknowledgements

First, and always, to my dear wife and partner, Anne. She has read and corrected this book as many times as I have, but with far more insight. I have been blessed all my life with the lack of judgment of beautiful women. I still am. Anne makes my life fun.

It is said that it is better to remain silent and be thought a fool than to speak and remove all doubt. This book would have removed all doubt if it had not been for my friend, Dr. Paul Tucker.

Paul was the Paul Hayes Tucker Distinguished Professor of Art at the University of Massachusetts, Boston (a chair created in his honor) and is a renowned art scholar. I admire him, as I do all of my successful friends who graduated from Yale, for their ability to overcome their educational deficiencies. Of course, he went to Williams as an undergraduate.

I would have come a cropper many a time if it hadn't been for Paul's knowledge. He corrected me and challenged me. He did it in detail and he was always right. Dang it. Any errors left over are mine, not his, I assure you. I am fortunate to have him as my friend.

Micalyn Harris has read all my books. Her thoughts and insights are always helpful. Her questions make me think. This book is better because of her. And what fortitude. She keeps coming back.

Elaine Kendall is a saint and a very well read one at that. Elaine, among other things, taught me the difference between "shamble" and "shambles."

And finally, but not at all the least, to Noah benShea, my wise buddy who graces me with his knowledge. Bless him.

www.ingramcontent.com/pod-product-compliance
Lightning Source LLC
Chambersburg PA
CBHW031419210526
45464CB00005B/1957